DEVIL'S DOORBELL

A John Treehorn Mystery

Dinah Miller

Contact:
New York Productions, LLC
P. O. Box 175
Churubusco, NY 12923

Cover Artwork by Leonie Cheetham
www.facebook.com/leoniecheethamart/

Please join my fan page for John Treehorn publishing news and updates.
www.facebook.com/SpecialAgentJohnTreehorn/

Line Editor: Jessica Keet
https://www.proofreadersproofreader.com

Line Editor: Annie Morgan
https://www.wordwolves.com

DEDICATION

You probably think this story is about you, don't you?

The priest kept a diary of confessions.

—FBI Special Agent John Treehorn

Chapter One

Death

One year ago

The drugstore's neon light cast a haunting illumination over the broken sidewalk that no one had taken the time or the effort to repair. Inside the store, the aging pharmacist glanced at the young, waif-like girl in front of him as he rang up her purchase. He opened his mouth to offer unsolicited advice but then observed a fellow church member watching. The professional placed her item into a paper bag and chose, at that moment, to stay silent.

The skinny girl kept her eyes lowered as she passed the owner, went out the door, and scurried down the front steps of the small-town store. Her long hair secured in a ponytail made her appear younger than her teenage years.

The shop owner's beady eyes watched her legs in their skinny jeans as she hurried away. He flipped the *Open* sign to *Closed* and watched her through the window.

The young girl, Cate, shoved the paper bag into the pocket of her hoodie and covered her head. Her cold fingers hugged the outerwear closer to her body as she tried in vain to absorb some warmth from it. Her holey sneakers filled with more dirt and pebbles as she walked again over the forgotten, broken sidewalk.

St. Philomena's Catholic Church, an old limestone structure with stained glass windows, glowed in the early evening light as the bells rang '*Onward, Christian Soldiers*' to beckon parishioners.

The girl picked up her pace even more, hurrying past the local diner as a State Police car slowly patrolled the area. She glanced at the vehicle. A single officer sat behind the wheel. Peering into the diner, she saw only a single customer perched on a stool.

"Pigs!"

Ahead, the mailbox painted *Janet Riley Foster Home #776* needed a new coat of black paint. Half of its letters had been destroyed by the elements. As Cate trudged across the weed-covered lawn bordering the diner's property she thought, *You'd think with the money they bring in from housing us kids, they could pay a gardener to clean up this mess!*

Before entering the house, she took one last look at the diner. A tremor rippled through her body. She knew she needed to make that call—the call for help. It was something that was as easy as breathing for some, but life-threatening for others.

Her hope that the television blaring in the living room would cover up the sound of her entering was short-lived.

"Cate, where have you been?"

"At the rectory," she lied.

"Your dinner's on the stove."

"Thanks."

She ignored the meal and hurried to her room. The thought of food made her gag as bile burned her throat.

Entering her plain bedroom, she kicked her homemade wedge beneath the door to keep everyone out.

Cate's hands shook as she tore open the packaging of the pregnancy test. She didn't bother reading the instructions but entered the bathroom and urinated on its white strip.

Two lines. Positive. She turned and vomited up the meager contents of her stomach.

Darkness crept into the room as night further encroached upon the village. The streetlamps clicked on one at a time, but failed to provide any illumination to the residents.

Cate prayed to the porcelain god as a deep coldness filled her soul She knew she had only one option. Returning to her room, she stripped her puke-covered clothes from her thin body, and slipped into an age-inappropriate, lacy negligee. Picking up her red lipstick, she wrote several words on her mirror. She reached beneath the lumpy mattress for the little hidden compartment and removed an item wrapped in white satin.

Then, she sat on the bed and waited. The little gold cross her mother had given her years earlier shone against her pale skin.

Her bedroom window slowly being opened caused the curtains to billow in the breeze. Someone had entered her room without her permission.

"Nice," whispered an older man's voice.

Cate Dixon raised her arm, pointed the gun at him, and uttered words that no sexual predator wanted to hear: "I'm pregnant."

The man's eyes widened as he recognized the revolver, comprehended the consequences of his assault, and immediately understood his DNA would condemn him to a prison cell.

Two individuals eyed the gun and its wooden-handled grip.

A single gun flash illuminated the bedroom window and the black of the moonless night as blood spattered against the teenager's wall.

This occurrence would shatter the not-so-peaceful, not-so-perfect little town.

Chapter Two

The Priest

Same town, present day

The streetlights illuminated the small town square. Some houses were darkened in sleep, while others glowed from the light of their televisions. A lone dog barked in the distance.

The man wondered whether he had disturbed the dog or if its ears were irritated by the church bells as they played a tune for the parishioners.

A leather-gloved hand opened the weathered, wooden church door. The man's soft-soled shoes silently crossed the aged, cracked floor tiles that were brought here long ago and skillfully laid by calloused men's hands.

Dim lights cast a softened glow over the pews. The stained glass window's patron saints looked down upon all who entered the holier-than-thou structure. Three rows of candles burned on a prayer table. The man thought the community needed more as the bells over his head rang out, *'Onward, Christian Soldier'*.

An index finger reached out and pressed the confessional booth bell. The man had nicknamed the button the *devil's doorbell*. Summon the devil and he will speak.

"Enter, my son," ordered Father Howard Bowden, a seventy-year-old, white-haired priest dressed in his black cleric robe with its obligatory white collar.

The parishioner calmly sat on the small built-in oak bench.

"May the Lord be in your heart to help you make a good confession."

The man's hand raised, aimed, and pulled the trigger of a wooden-handled gun. Passing through the confessional screen, the bullet struck the priest squarely in the forehead. The pungent odor of gunpowder permeated the small cubicle as the shooter pocketed the weapon. Then, he stepped effortlessly out of his cubicle and entered the cleric's space.

Blood oozed from the fatal wound as the priest sat, slumped against the oak-paneled wall of his confessional booth. A little bit of life in the gravity of depravity dripped down his nose to the corner of his mouth as if it wanted to issue a warning—but no lies would ever be spoken again.

The killer removed a plastic bag that contained a written note and a knife. His arms made quick movements on the victim but his activity remained hidden.

The murderer then slipped quietly out of the booth and the front door of the building. Not a single person, here on Earth, witnessed his exit from the gray stone church or the purposeful stride that took him to a secondary task that awaited him at the rectory.

The morning sunrise cast a warm glow over the leaded glass windows of the Arts and Crafts bungalow. The fireplace's ashes sat cold, no longer emanating any of the warmth of the previous evening. The aroma wafting from the coffee pot slowly woke the man. A book that had garnered his attention the night before now lay on the floor where it had dropped from his fingers when he had fallen asleep in front of the fire.

As he filled his second cup of coffee the police radio beeped and a dispatcher broke the peaceful morning, "All cars, code 187. There's been a murder at St. Philomena's Catholic Church, on the Main Square in Altona. All cars please respond."

Captain Thomas Brook's hand reached out and turned off the radio. His telephone rang at the same time as his cuckoo clock chimed.

"Hello."

"I need you on this one."

"No, Mr. Major."

"I *could* order you, you know?"

"I've never taken an order from you before. Why would I start now?"

They both laughed.

"I've never had to *give* you an order. You've always known your job. The Governor said he would grant you a favor if this case gets solved."

"That's big of him."

"Then do it for me."

Neither man spoke.

"The Governor will owe me a favor?"

"That's what he said. He's Catholic and he wants this solved."

"I heard it on the radio. Who's dead at the church?"

"The priest."

"That's federal land."

"I spoke with your friend... Mister FBI Director Andrew Mason himself. The Feds are sending an agent to head up the investigation. He'll take the lead on the priest's murder since it happened on federal land. You'll take the lead on the second murder which occurred on state property."

"Who's the other victim?"

"The priest's housekeeper, Loveta Chilton. Her body was found at the rectory."

"I'm on my way."

"Thanks, Thomas."

"I'll earn that favor."

Thomas walked to his closet and grabbed his New York State Police Captain's uniform. It was time for him to return to the job.

Washington DC

FBI Special Agent John Treehorn stopped for the red light at the intersection of Church and State on the outskirts of Georgetown, watching as morning commuters navigated the crosswalk holding their briefcases and hot drinks.

The news on the radio caught the agent's attention: *"Indian Times reporter Jori Lansing reporting. Wonderful news out of Tucson. Ex-ATF Asst. Director Colin Finch's wife, Bethany, and their two daughters were dropped off overnight at St. Philomena's Catholic Church by unknown assailants. Mrs. Finch stated she and her daughters were unharmed in Mexico and the family requests privacy at this time. There is no word on the whereabouts of Colin Finch, who has an outstanding arrest warrant for entering Mexico without the court's permission after his recent federal arrest."*

Treehorn's cellphone beeped with a personal text tone that to a stranger sounded like someone's nose being smashed. The agent's lip curled as he pressed his 'listen' button.

"Hello, my mojito. Your packages were delivered as your fists requested. You owe me a favor, my friend."

The thirty-five-year-old Navajo's bruised knuckles whitened as he clenched the steering wheel. He knew no favor would be forthcoming. He didn't need to look in the mirror to see the week-old fading bruises beneath his blue/brown heterochromic eye, or the two catgut stitches his black eyebrow partially concealed. The only satisfaction Treehorn felt was that he was returning to work today, and CIA Agent Shady Lynch required another week to recuperate from the injuries he had sustained during their fistfight.

Treehorn's finger hesitated over his dash button but then he finally pressed it, "Call Sam."

The phone rang once and she picked it up. "Dr. Samantha Reynolds."

"I know you have my ID on your phone."

"Is this a professional or personal call, Mr. Treehorn?"

The Fed's bruised jaw clenched in pain as he said, "It's Special Agent John Treehorn."

"You didn't answer my question, *Agent Treehorn*."

"Samantha," he said, his voice softening to his lover, "It's been a week. Are you going to let me explain?"

"I take that as personal. So, let me make it very clear. From now on, you're only to contact me on official FBI business. *Do you understand*? We're done!"

"Sam…" the widowed FBI agent whispered to the second woman he ever loved, "Let's talk about it."

The phone clicked, giving him an unwanted answer.

As the light turned green, Treehorn's phone rang. His heart hoped it was her but instead it was his supervisor, FBI Assistant Director Leo Mancuso.

"John Treehorn."

"Mancuso. Do you want a murder investigation or the welcome back party that's waiting for you?"

"Where's the murder?"

Mancuso chuckled.

"Upstate New York. Two deceased: one on an Indian territory, the other off. Plane's waiting at Reagan. Patricia's sending you the file."

"Anything I need to know?"

"I'll send you a rover to assist on the FBI side. You'll be partnered with Thomas Brooks, State Police. Treehorn, he's friends with the Director. They graduated together from the Academy."

"Why send me?"

"He didn't want to pull any agents off the drugs or immigration problems along the northern border. Small isolated town. Crime occurred on a little piece of federal land. The victim's a priest. You're a lawyer. Mason thought you'd be a good fit."

"The Church won't give up its secrets."

"Exactly. Search for the truth. Hey, you never know. The director may look kindly upon you for once if you help his friend find the killer," Mancuso joked.

"I want the Jules Rathburn case."

Mancuso's humor quickly evaporated as he replied, "It's out of my hands."

He terminated the call before his agent could argue.

Treehorn activated his siren and emergency lights. He had a plane to catch.

Sitting in the departure lounge, Treehorn read the file that arrived via email from Patricia, Mancuso's administrative assistant. Then he telephoned his friend and colleague, Special Agent Raven Shelly, at the FBI office in Gallup, New Mexico and left a message on his voicemail.

"Treehorn here. I'm emailing you a new case of mine. Can you do a background profile on the individuals listed in the files I send? I'm flying to Plattsburgh. Keep this private and secure."

The agent's lip curled as he forwarded Raven the information. If anyone had observed him at that split second, they would have pitied the people he hunted.

Altona, New York

New York State Police vehicles, coroner, and criminal investigation SUVs lined the road outside St. Philomena's

Catholic Church. A yellow police ribbon circled the structure and its rectory.

Exiting his unmarked cruiser, Thomas surveyed the activity. Everyone had a job to do and they all appeared to be doing it thoroughly.

As he ducked under the ribbon, he rubbed it between his fingers. Someone had crossed the line here to commit murder. The State Trooper looked at the gray quarried stone church with its slate roof. He hoped it wasn't strong enough to hold its religious secrets. He paused upon entering the vestibule so his eyes could adjust and the staff inside could acknowledge his presence.

A calmness settled over the staff after they recognized the return of their commanding officer, Thomas Brooks. At age fifty, he stood tall and authoritative with his short, dark hair that was graying slightly at the temples. His New York State Police uniform decorated with a two-silver-bar pin determined his rank of Captain above all. He paused at the holy water vessel, observed his reflection, and then flicked it with his middle finger.

Several members of the Crime Scene Unit watched him, but quickly returned to their assigned duties before he could see their directed gazes. Their old boss had finally returned to the job.

As Captain Brooks entered the building, NYS Policeman Doug Milner, a youthful thirty-year-old, glanced at his partner, Rita Holmes, a same-age officer on the fast track to becoming an investigator.

"I never expected to see God here," Trooper Milner whispered.

"Captain Thomas Brooks!" Trooper Holmes said with a smile.

"I thought he retired?"

"Medical leave," she informed him.

"Why do you think he's here?"

"It's elementary, Trooper Milner. He's here to solve the crime."

Both of the officers straightened, nodding respectfully to their direct supervisor.

"Milner, Holmes."

"Captain."

"Welcome back, sir!"

Trooper Holmes pointed to the wooden structure.

"Father Bowden's body is in the confessional booth."

"The FBI's sending one Special Agent John Treehorn. Can you keep an eye out for him?"

The pair nodded.

17

The captain walked past the pews, ignoring the beauty of the church as he aimed straight for the pair of confessional booths. He always thought the holy structure could have used more.

A slightly overweight, fair-haired male dressed in a Crime Scene Unit uniform muttered to himself, "Who would kill a priest?"

Captain Brooks took one look at the body and answered, "Someone with a gun."

The kneeling guy smiled and turned toward him.

"Welcome back, sir. We don't need to tell you how…"

The captain held up his hand to stop the man mid-sentence. "Save the speech. What do we have here, Harris?"

The technician stepped aside so Brooks could see the victim. Blood covered the priest's head.

"Cause of death other than the obvious?"

"Single gunshot to the head. Approximate time of death: ten pm."

"Why the excessive blood smear?"

"Occurred postmortem. The killer removed an eye, ear, and part of the man's tongue."

"He was involved in a situation he shouldn't have been."

"Why do you assume that?"

"Buddha. See no evil, hear no evil, speak no evil."

Harris handed the captain a labeled evidence bag containing a blood-stained note.

Thomas examined it closely. It appeared to be the top half of a torn page.

"Where did you find this?"

"It was stabbed to the priest's heart, postmortem."

The man read the fine cursive print dated from the day before, *"I have committed a crime. A crime against my God, my church, and my community. Please forgive me."*

As he returned the item to Agent Harris he asked, "Would it have been too much to ask for the killer to have signed it?"

"What, and make our jobs easier?"

"Did the major arrive?"

"He's next door at the rectory."

Troopers Holmes and Milner watched as Thomas exited the church.

Holmes whispered to her partner, "He solved a large percentage of his cases when he wore his investigator's hat."

"Now he wears Captain's silver bars."

"They say he and the major rose up the ranks together. That's why he was so successful. The major had his back for years, allowing him to work the cases in his own style but still within the confines of the law."

"How did he end up here?"

"Altona? He was born and raised here. He knows all of the characters in this game, Milner."

"Then the odds are in our favor that this case will be solved."

The Troopers butted fists and smiled.

Captain Brooks slowly walked along the yellow police ribbon to the rectory, a plain white, two-story structure with the same matching slate roof. The house sat over a hundred feet from the stone church. Highly unlikely that the housekeeper had heard the gunfire from her location.

Police officers and staff stepped aside as the captain entered the porch.

At age fifty-five, New York State Police Major Steven Morgan stood as tall and distinguished as Captain Brooks in his uniform. He watched as his subordinate scanned the area.

Questions filled each of their investigative minds. Major Morgan addressed the professionals nearest to them, asking, "Would you excuse us?"

The staff moved professionally away, nodding respectfully to the two commanding officers. One of them closed the front door of the house to give the two men privacy.

"Captain."

"Major."

"Thomas."

"Steven."

The younger man saluted the older. "Reporting for duty, sir."

"Don't *sir* me."

"Yes, sir. No, sir."

The two men shook hands as they chuckled.

"What brought you up north?" Thomas asked.

"A meeting. I postponed my return trip to Albany today when the call came in. Has the Fed shown up yet?"

Thomas shook his head.

"He should be here soon. I hope he doesn't get in my way."

"Are you turning away help?"

"I'm not stupid," remarked the captain, "Sometimes they don't send the sharpest pencil in the box."

Major Morgan nodded.

"Who would kill a priest?" He didn't expect an answer.

"Someone with a gun and a motive."

The two State Policemen watched the younger, dedicated staff work the second crime scene.

"Thomas, you'll need a doctor's order to return."

The captain removed a paper from his uniform pocket and flicked his wrist to open it.

"Return to work, sir. The doctor signed it three months ago."

The major glanced at the document.

"I know. He called me the day he recorded it in your file." On a more serious note, "Are you going to have any trouble working with the Fed?"

"I'll make sure he knows where he stands."

"The FBI's sending Special Agent John Treehorn. One of their best investigators. Are you prepared to answer his questions?"

"I'll tell him what he needs to know."

"The sooner these cases are closed, the sooner he'll depart," his friend and Major advised.

"I'll remember that."

"Congratulations, this murder is yours. The Feds have the priest. Good luck working together. No witness or apparent motive."

Thomas smirked as he said, "You can ask the killer when he's caught."

Major Morgan chuckled as he added, "Your friend FBI Director Mason and I placed a little friendly wager on you and their agent as to who'll solve his murder first."

"What's the prize?"

His supervisor didn't offer an answer.

"By the way, the governor's Catholic, it's an election year, and he's betting that you'll solve this crime."

"I'll work hard to earn that favor from him."

"You do that."

As he climbed into his unmarked SUV and drove away, Thomas watched his loyal friend and boss look around the area from where he stood. The pharmacy, church, rectory, diner, and foster care home. So much pain and suffering with too many secrets just waiting to be exposed.

Chapter Three

Special Agent

FBI Special Agent John Treehorn climbed into the driver's seat of the black Chevy Tahoe that awaited his arrival at Plattsburgh International Airport. His telephone received a call and he connected it to the vehicle's Bluetooth.

"I just arrived in Plattsburgh but you already knew that by my tracking," Treehorn remarked, stating the obvious to his fellow FBI agent stationed in Gallup.

"Your point?" Raven joked and then turned serious, "I've kept this search private and secured."

Treehorn's lips pursed as he said, "You'll understand why, one day."

"Too late. The database provided the answer to my curiosity."

The agent needed to know what was uncovered; then, he would know how to protect his friend and partner.

"What did you find?"

Raven listed the detailed information he'd located in the short amount of time. He then enlightened Treehorn on both Thomas Brooks' professional and personal history.

This time Treehorn's lip curled in disdain. He wasn't a betting man, but the agent knew he wouldn't have been assigned to this case if FBI Director Mason had known of the surprising detail that Raven had just exposed.

The senior agent issued a brief order: "Delete the complete search and history."

"Already did that before we spoke."

Treehorn had assumed this would be a straightforward investigation, but now he knew otherwise.

The drive from Plattsburgh to the crime scene was a short commute. Altona—with a population of just under three thousand—had one stop light, contained one church, and a tiny square made up of approximately fifty homes. The rest of the residences were scattered over a hundred square miles. As he drove around the town square's perimeter, homeowners openly stared as he slowly drove past them. This was the type of community that recognized a stranger in their midst.

Supposedly, the teenager's suicide a year ago at the local foster care home rocked this quaint, little God-loving town. He doubted that after listening to Raven's report.

Treehorn parked his SUV next to the County Coroner's vehicle in the church parking lot.

Next door was the local diner, full of watchful eyes focusing their attention on the crime scene's newest arrival. As the tall agent exited his vehicle, his short, black FBI regulation haircut shone like a beacon statement: a stranger stood among them.

Treehorn felt the hairs on the back of his neck stand up as his ingrained, law enforcement training kicked in. He searched for and found all of the eyes at the diner trained on him, not out of curiosity but with something resembling fear.

From the rectory's porch, Thomas watched the agent's stance and the citizens' reactions to him.

Treehorn lifted his jacket and placed his hand on his hip, showing every set of eyes that were focused on him his gold badge and pistol. He took his time examining their faces, waiting until each and every one of them had turned away.

Thomas chuckled and decided to wait for the Fed to make his appearance at the rectory.

The dead body wasn't moving until the coroner concluded his work so he decided he could wait for the man's arrival.

Treehorn followed the coroner's staff into the church as they wheeled in their gurney.

Examining the interior of the church, the agent found numerous law enforcement officers, LEOs, performing their duties.

The staff and CSU Harris watched the Fed's arrival and all of them now gained a closer look at the man.

In his mid-thirties, FBI Special Agent John Treehorn stood six foot tall, half Navajo, half white, with a short, black FBI regulation haircut and a tanned complexion. But it was the man's eyes that stood out. Heterochromic, with a brown iris on the outer rims and a blue one on the inner. Not too lean but muscular enough to win a fight and by the looks of the bruises on the man's face, proof someone had fought with him very recently.

The Crime Scene Unit staff member removed his latex glove and held his hand out to the agent, observing his bruised knuckles and face.

"CSU Harris, New York State Police. How did the other man fare?"

Presenting his identification Treehorn replied coolly, "FBI Special Agent John Treehorn. He's still on medical leave."

"Good to know," Harris said with a chuckle, "Have you met Trooper's Holmes and Milner?"

The three law enforcement officers nodded in acknowledgement.

"Hey, Doc. Fed's here!"

Harris pointed to the confessional booth.

A short, white-haired man turned around from where he was standing over the corpse. One hand held a camera while the other held a blood-covered liver thermometer.

Treehorn showed his ID to the coroner.

"FBI Special Agent John Treehorn."

"Elliot Spencer, Clinton County Coroner."

"What do we have, Doc?"

"Harris did the preliminary liver temp earlier. A two-victim fatality this morning slowed my arrival. Take a look."

The coroner pointed to the body as he deposited the contaminated instrument into a hazardous waste safety bag.

"Father Howard Bowden. COD, a .40 caliber, single gunshot to the head. One exit wound. Bullet is lodged in the panel. Approximate time of death, ten pm. His facial disfigurement occurred postmortem. Someone removed an eye, ear, and part of the man's tongue. They left the knife as a souvenir."

CSU Harris added, "The shot came from the adjoining confessional."

He handed Treehorn the evidence bag containing a blood-covered, torn page.

"This was found stabbed to the priest's chest."

The agent examined the slip of paper and returned it to the technician.

Eyeing the dead priest's bloodied face, Treehorn said, "Buddha. See no evil, hear no evil, speak no evil."

"Wow! Captain Brooks said the same. He's next door at the rectory with the second body."

Pulling his business card from his pocket, Treehorn handed it to the coroner and said, "My contact information."

"Thanks, I'll call you when I have the official results."

Thomas watched from the porch as the Federal agent's long legs walked toward him. The man carried his authority well.

Treehorn knew the officer was waiting for him but he intentionally stopped to take the necessary time to examine the crime scene locations. He then proceeded to the enclosed porch to meet the man who had waited patiently for him since he exited his vehicle. Treehorn's observation skills never missed the details. The Fed briefly examined the man's uniform as if it were consequential to the investigation. He held out his hand, stating, "FBI Special Agent John Treehorn."

The trooper shook the man's strong grip as he replied, "Captain Thomas Brooks, New York State Police. You can call me Thomas."

"Treehorn. Friends with the director?"

The man didn't beat around the bush.

Up close, the captain realized his friend in Washington had sent an Indian to investigate.

Interesting.

"Yes, but don't worry, I won't run to him if you screw up."

Treehorn squinted at the trooper.

"I have no problem removing you from this case if you can't keep up."

Thomas chuckled. Treehorn didn't.

"Where's the second body in this joint investigation?"

"Living room. Let me introduce you."

The men signed into the police log and entered the crime scene.

The two men examined the rectory's foyer which led

directly to the dining room. Off to the right was the kitchen and to the left, the living room where everyone appeared to be gathered.

Treehorn observed the interior: it was like a time capsule from the 1950s.

"May I please have your attention? I'm Captain Thomas Brooks and I'm now in charge of the state's investigation: the murder of Loveta Chilton. This is FBI Special Agent John Treehorn who will head Father Bowden's federal case. The two agencies will work jointly to solve these crimes."

The group acknowledged the men with respectful nods as a voice in the rear added, "Welcome back!"

Treehorn didn't question the response aimed at his peer. He already knew its reason.

The two men approached CSU Gerry Mullens, a thirty-something, short-haired female dressed in blue overalls with 'CSU' labeled on her back. Her dedicated focus stayed on the body.

Treehorn examined the location of the pajama-clad female sprawled in front of and hidden by the sofa. The victim appeared to be in her mid-60's, a grey-haired woman with a single gunshot to the center of her forehead. She had been aware of her imminent death and by her clothing knew the perpetrator.

"What do you have, Gerry?"

"Loveta Chilton. The priest's live-in secretary, cook, and housekeeper. She was killed here with a high probability from that weapon."

An antique, wooden-handled revolver lay next to the victim.

"It holds five cartridges. Three bullets have been fired from it."

"Is there a third victim?"

"The troopers secured both properties and only found two bodies."

"Any sign of a break-in or robbery?"

"No, but both properties are open to community residents at all times and nothing appears to have been stolen."

"Who found the bodies?"

"Sarah Sawyer, local resident and part-time cleaner. She found the priest and panicked. Ran here. That's when she found the housekeeper and telephoned the police."

The sound of a woman crying came from the rear of the house.

"Ms. Sawyer's in the den waiting to be questioned."

Treehorn nodded.

"Was there any bad employment history with Ms. Chilton?"

"None that we know of at this point. The priest employed her for years."

"Has the rectory been searched for the diary?" Thomas asked CSU Mullens.

"Yes, but no book or journal has been located with a page similar to what was found on Father Bowden's body."

Questioning its significance, Treehorn asked, "The killer may have brought the page with him."

Thomas countered, "Or removed a page from it before stealing it."

"Possibly."

Mullens continued, "If we set aside the diary, murder appears to be the only crime that occurred here. There are antiques, money, and medication—all untouched."

Treehorn looked at Thomas.

"Father Bowden was the target. That much is clear from the condition of his body. Someone had a personal agenda to address."

"Agreed."

"The housekeeper may have known the killer."

"Or his motive," Thomas added.

"Or witnessed the murder…"

"I'm sure one of you will solve this," CSU Mullens said, assessing the two investigators as they interpreted the crime scene.

Thomas looked at Treehorn with his eyebrow raised as if to ask, *Which one?*

Treehorn's facial features remained stoic, "It's not a competition."

"I'm sorry. I d-d-didn't mean it like that," the woman stuttered.

"My contact information has been logged in."

As Treehorn turned and walked away, Thomas whispered to his tech: "FBI, they're a different breed. Keep us updated with any results on the investigation."

"As always."

The trooper watched as Treehorn entered the darkened hallway and disappeared from his sight. Thomas believed the killer made a mistake by murdering the priest on Federal land, thus involving the FBI in this case.

Sarah Sawyer's red, tear-stained face highlighted the woman's trauma. Her sobs quieted to whimpers as the two men entered the room. The woman's blond disheveled hair defined her day.

Treehorn pressed his white monogrammed

handkerchief into the woman's hand. She repeatedly tried to keep her tangled hair back from her face.

"What's happening in this town? Last year, that poor girl's suicide and now this."

The two officers, dressed in suits and standing against the back wall, glanced at their Captain. They appeared uncomfortable as their eyes shifted from their supervisor to the female.

Treehorn spoke first, "I'm FBI Special Agent John Treehorn. I'm sorry for the trauma you experienced finding the victims."

"These are New York State Police Investigators Edward Ryan and Christopher Barnett."

The two men nodded.

"Agent Treehorn will be the lead investigator for Father Bowden and I'll be covering Ms. Chilton's case in this joint investigation."

The younger man handed Thomas a metal clipboard with a completed document attached.

"We've collected her basic information."

"We'll take it from here," Treehorn said. He noticed both troopers relax once they knew they could step back from questioning the witness.

Thomas stepped up.

"Can you please tell us what you saw from the beginning?"

Sarah wiped her eyes and began, "I was assigned to the church this morning so I arrived on time. The door was unlocked as usual. I found Father Bowden in the confessional booth as I walked toward the closet for my cleaning supplies."

"Did you see anyone outside of the church?"

Sarah shook her head.

"Anyone inside?"

"No, no one."

"Did you notice anything out of the ordinary?"

"No. Everything was exactly where it should have been—except for the dead guy. I found the priest and then I immediately ran from the church to the rectory as fast as I could. The church office was locked so I went next door to use the phone. That's when I found Loveta."

"Is the church office usually locked?"

"Yes."

"What happened next?" Thomas asked.

Sarah became agitated and clenched the handkerchief.

Treehorn softly encouraged her, "Take your time."

"I came in search of Loveta to tell her and call the police. That's when I found my friend."

"I'm sorry for your loss. When did you last see her alive?"

"Last night after mass. We returned here for coffee."

Sarah glanced at Thomas but focused on Treehorn.

"The service didn't go well. Something had upset the priest. He yelled at the whole congregation and then pointed his fingers at the so-called-pillars of our community, calling them sinners of this town."

"Did he mention anyone specifically?"

Sarah nodded.

"I've never seen him act like that. I think something was medically wrong. He shouted and waved his bible. Several residents stood up and walked out."

"We'll need the names of those individuals and any statements you can remember."

"Do you think there's a killer among us?"

Eyeing the agitated woman, Treehorn answered kindly, "We'll do our best to find the answer."

Then Thomas asked a question that all investigators voice: "Is there anything else you know that may assist us in this investigation?"

"Loveta told me he received an upsetting call last night before mass."

"Did she tell you who telephoned?"

"No, but Loveta said she overheard the conversation. Father Bowden shouted this to the caller, *"I did a terrible thing. I lied for you once—never again!"*

She said he slammed down the phone and hurried out of the rectory for the service."

"Did you see him at the church?"

Sarah nodded and wiped her tears.

"He yelled and called me a lazy sloth. I thought I did the same job as the last cleaner but I was wrong. I returned here and Loveta comforted me. She felt he had directed his anger toward me because there was no one else around."

Treehorn waited for this opportunity and asked, "One last question, Ms. Sawyer. What girl's suicide did you reference?"

Thomas gasped.

Treehorn heard it. Then he watched Sarah's eyes widen and lower to avoid contact.

"Agent Treehorn, my daughter, Cate, died a year ago," Thomas answered coldly.

Treehorn's expressionless eyes met Thomas' glare. The Fed didn't pursue the subject.

"Here's my card, Ms. Sawyer. If there's anything you remember, please give me a call."

"I'm quitting. Can I leave now? I'm not coming back here."

"We ask that you finish your statement and leave your contact information." Treehorn requested.

Thomas added, "I'll leave you with Investigator Ryan to work on the details. List as many names as you can remember from last night's mass and Father Bowden's statements. It may help with these investigations."

"Trooper Barnett, I'd like a word with you."

Treehorn watched the troopers follow their Captain's orders. They respected him.

The three LEOs moved to the living room where they found Loveta's corpse encased in a black body bag being transported on a gurney out of the front door by the coroner's staff.

Thomas ordered Investigator Ryan, "When Barnett is finished, I want you two to interview these "*sinners of the community*", get their contact information, and especially what they said. Agent Treehorn and I will re-interview the ones that have information pertinent to these cases."

The officer examined his watch.

Thomas gave his colleague a hard stare.

"Do you think the priest or his housekeeper have the time?"

"Sorry, sir."

"I want you two to change into your grey uniforms to conduct the interviews. Drive a cruiser, too."

"Sir?" Investigator Ryan questioned his supervisor.

"I want everyone in this town to know who's being interviewed."

The officer nodded. "We'll get right on it."

The Fed raised his stitched eyebrow but remained silent.

"Do you have anything you wish to add, Agent Treehorn?"

"I have some background questions for you."

"Can I answer them over a cup of coffee?"

The agent examined the time on his watch, nodding once.

"Yes."

As the pair exited the rectory, Treehorn took a long, hard look at the stone cold church behind him.

Chapter Four

Calling Winter LaGrange

As Thomas and Treehorn entered the diner, all the conversations ceased.

Delores the waitress, or so her name tag said, asked with purpose, "Coffee, Thomas?"

Thomas raised two fingers to the woman. She nodded.

"Have a seat, gentlemen, and I'll be right back."

"I'll be right back, too," Thomas said to Treehorn as he headed toward the restroom sign.

Delores poured the hot drinks and delivered them to the booth.

"The menus are there with today's specials."

"Thanks. Just coffee," Treehorn supplied.

"New in town?" the waitress asked, eyeing his gun, gold badge, and Native American heritage.

"FBI."

"Good luck!" she chuckled as she resumed her work.

Treehorn, who never sat with his back to the door, watched as the customers glanced at him, quickly paid their bills, and rushed out of the establishment.

As customers continued to exit the diner, a woman entered, located the Special Agent, and slid into his booth.

"Scaring customers away?"

Treehorn eyed the young Navajo woman as he said, "Special Agent Melanie Hopper."

"Did you just offer me congratulations on my new rank?"

Treehorn squinted at her. She was one of the youngest agents ever to gain special agent status yet he offered no response.

"Mancuso let it slip that you recommended me for the promotion."

Treehorn's lip curled.

"Mancuso never lets anything slip."

Melanie smirked.

"Whereas, I did inform him that you now owe Shady Lynch a favor."

The humor immediately disappeared from Special Agent Hopper's face.

"You've learned nothing from me!" Treehorn stated tersely.

"That's not true."

"Good luck proving otherwise. Remember this conversation because, when the time comes and Shady calls in that favor you granted him, you'll pay for it for the rest of your life."

"Is that what happened to you? Is that what drives you? A mistake?"

"My only regret is not seeing the truth when it stared me in the face."

"Thanks for the whipping and coffee," she said as she sipped the drink.

"Have you read the case?"

"No. Boss man ordered me here. I figured you'd get to the point as soon as I arrived."

"One dead priest murdered on Federal land. His housekeeper's body was found on state property. Captain Thomas Brooks of the New York State Police heads their investigation."

"Plan on shooting anyone while you're here?"

"No. My goal is to identify the killer asap so I can transfer to another investigation."

"Whose case?"

"Jules Rathburn."

"You ever wonder why you haven't been assigned to it?"

Treehorn glanced at his fellow agent as Thomas appeared next to their booth.

"Am I interrupting?"

Treehorn answered, his gaze remaining fixed on his junior agent, "Yes, but it can wait."

"Hello," Thomas greeted the woman.

Melanie looked up at the uniform and flushed.

"May I sit here?" Thomas asked.

Melanie slid over and moved her coffee cup too.

"Can I assume I'm drinking yours?"

Thomas winked at Melanie as he said, "My lips didn't touch it, if that's a concern."

Treehorn watched their interaction without commenting.

Melanie glanced at her partner whose only movement was a raised, stitched eyebrow. The female agent flushed, again.

Since Treehorn offered no introduction, the captain held out his hand and said, "Thomas Brooks, New York State Police."

"FBI Special Agent Melanie Hopper."

"Welcome aboard. Please call me Thomas."

Delores interrupted by delivering another cup of coffee to the trooper.

"Can I get you all something to eat?"

Answering for everyone Treehorn replied, "No thanks. Just coffee."

Delores got the message. They didn't want to be disturbed.

"I'm sure glad I ate before I arrived!" Melanie snapped.

"I see your flippant attitude hasn't changed. I thought your last assailant would have beaten it out of you."

"I see yours failed to adjust you."

Thomas chuckled at the two. "Lovers?"

"No!" Melanie answered for both.

Treehorn's lip curled in distaste.

"She's not my type."

Melanie leaned forward as she said snarkily, "*No one's* your type."

"I'm the senior agent here, don't forget it," Treehorn stated coldly.

"You never let me…" Melanie wise-cracked.

Thomas watched the man's face lose all emotion as he went in for the kill.

Treehorn whispered, "Do me a *favor*?"

Thomas saw Melanie flinch and sit back while Treehorn leaned forward and said, "Do your job."

The two agents stared at each other. Neither surrendering.

Thomas realized the agents were two sides of a coin.

"Did your boss have an agenda when he sent you here?"

Treehorn's face pinched in anger.

"Tell me about your daughter's suicide," he asked, changing the subject.

Melanie heard Thomas gasp. Score one for the senior Navajo agent.

"Self-inflicted gunshot wound. Age fourteen. Investigation went dead. I took a leave of absence."

Thomas glanced at Melanie and continued, "This is my first case since I got back." His eyes returned to Treehorn. "End of story."

"Where's her mother?" Treehorn pressed.

"Killed in a car accident."

Melanie placed her hand on the trooper's arm as she said sympathetically, "I'm so sorry."

Thomas met her warm eyes.

"It's all in the past."

Delores approached with a full coffee pot and asked, "Refill anyone?"

Three cups were pushed toward the woman.

Waiting until she was out of earshot Treehorn asked, "Tell me about this town."

"Small town, rural living. Majority of residents travel to Plattsburgh for work. Altona State Correctional Facility is down the road. Generational farmers and small business-owners make up the rest. A town where everyone knows everyone's business."

"Why do you think the priest and housekeeper were murdered?"

"The priest lived and worked in this community for over forty years. He's kept a lot of secrets. If the slip of paper found on his body is any indication, then he wrote some down."

"You're assuming it's his diary?" Treehorn countered.

Melanie interrupted, "The priest kept a diary of confessions?"

"A torn page was stabbed to the man's body. We're waiting for handwriting analysis."

"The diary appeared to be the only thing missing from the rectory, if that's where it was kept."

"My men are conducting a thorough search to verify any other possible stolen items."

Melanie added, "The community won't appreciate that their dirty, little secrets were recorded for posterity."

"They won't take kindly to them being released, either," Thomas added.

"I think the priest covered up more than a secret; I think he covered up a crime."

He repeated Sarah Sawyer's statement about the priest's telephone conversation when he said, *"I did a terrible thing. I lied for you once—never again!"*

"What if he detailed the crime in his diary?" Melanie theorized.

"Then we'll be looking for someone seeking revenge."

"Or, someone who wants its information to be released to the public."

Treehorn tilted his head a fraction. Melanie recognized the look on her partner's face as he processed this information.

"Or both?" she asked.

Thomas tapped his porcelain cup.

"There's one thing at the rectory that's bothered me," he said, challenging the Fed's investigative skills.

Treehorn didn't disappoint. "The gun. Why leave it?"

"I think it has a history that needs to be exposed. We should have its ballistics and the coroner's report first thing tomorrow. I've ordered a conference room to be set up at our station for you, and my staff will be at your full disposal."

Melanie watched the two men partner up.

"When do you plan on interviewing Loveta's daughter, Winter LaGrange?"

"As soon as you finish your coffee."

Thomas emptied his cup and handed Melanie a clean napkin. He tapped the corner of his mouth.

"You missed a spot," he said with a wink.

"Thanks!" Melanie smiled.

Treehorn frowned as he dropped money on the table.

"Hopper, ride with me. We have FBI business to discuss."

Loveta Chilton gave birth to one child, Winter LaGrange, a childless widow. Her husband, Luke, an accountant, drove home one snowy winter's night and didn't survive an icy car crash.

Treehorn noticed an outpouring of support from friends and neighbors upon their arrival at her small, wooden-clad home.

The women carried plenty of covered dishes and beverages. The panacea of grief.

Thomas joined the group and lifted the heavier items. These were his community members too.

Treehorn glanced at Melanie and said, "Go help them."

"Because it's *women's* work?"

"Have I ever mistreated you or any female in a misogynistic way?"

"You just did."

Treehorn shook his head.

"You misunderstood. I just figured they would be more willing to open up to a female FBI agent. That chip on your shoulder must be mighty heavy at times. *Do your job*."

"I'm sorry."

"Start acting like an FBI agent or I'll have a discussion with Mancuso."

"Yes, sir," Melanie saluted him.

Treehorn turned away without commenting, but Melanie didn't miss his clenched jaw. She knew he wouldn't let her forget the misstep.

Following Treehorn's orders, Melanie engaged with a group of women while he followed an elderly couple into the home's front entrance without knocking. It didn't take long to find the victim's daughter.

"Winter LaGrange?"

She nodded.

"FBI Special Agent John Treehorn," he stated, presenting her with his identification, "Is there somewhere we can talk in private?"

"We can use my den."

Treehorn followed the woman, who appeared to be in her late thirties. He had long since lost track of the number of grieving souls he had encountered over the years.

"Captain Thomas is the lead investigator on your mother's case while I'm handling Father Bowden's. Would you like to wait for him? He'll probably ask you the same questions."

"No, I can answer you separately."

"Please tell me your mother's history at the rectory."

"When my dad passed away, my mom was hired. It was a live-in position so it helped with her retirement and cut down on expenses."

"How long was she employed?"

"Over ten years. She hired Sarah to help out when the previous cleaner, Betty Luzer, died."

"Was Father Bowden a good employer?"

"Yes. My mom said he lived the life of a priest. Kind and giving. The community loved him. And then, one day it changed."

"What happened?"

"My mom told me it started over a year ago. She said he would receive some late-night calls that he'd take in his private office. The priest would start yelling but being the good Catholic, she would stay in her room until he quieted."

"Could she identify the caller?"

"No. The priest had a separate telephone line installed for confidentiality."

"Is there anything else?"

"My mom would also help out home-bound elderly in the area. It was the part of the priest's community advocacy that she enjoyed the most, but in that position, she developed a keen awareness of age-related illnesses. A little over a year ago the priest had a serious argument with someone. The next day he showed confusion. Mom believes that's when he started to exhibit signs of dementia."

"The coroner will have access to his medical records for the autopsy."

Wondering what prevented Thomas from joining his interview, Treehorn asked, "When was the last time you saw or spoke with your mother?"

"Mom called me yesterday. She told me the priest was losing it and she was going to call someone for help but didn't say who. She whispered to me that he repeated people's confessions, which really upset her."

"That's understandable. It's a sacred sacrament."

"She messaged me a couple of times at work. Nothing secret. Just his behavior."

"Can I see those messages?"

Winter nodded.

"I called her before I left work and said I would drop off some groceries later that night at the rectory. She told me she was going to bed and to just leave them in the kitchen. I do that all of the time. It wasn't unusual."

"Did you see her?"

"No, Agent Treehorn. I went to the bathroom and realized I'd forgotten my medication. I grabbed my stuff and drove home. I didn't check on her because I figured she was sleeping. The rectory was quiet."

"What time?"

"Shortly after 10 pm."

Treehorn didn't comment.

"Was she dead by then?"

"We'll wait for the coroner's report."

Treehorn didn't want her to know what he suspected. The killer may have been inside the house murdering her mother while she was there.

"Let me show you the messages my mom sent me about the priest."

She retrieved her phone from her purse.

Treehorn watched Thomas and Melanie deep in conversation outside while he waited for Loveta's daughter to return.

Winter sat down and turned on her telephone's power. She typed in its four-digit code but the screen stated, 'Invalid.'

"That's odd. My password doesn't work."

She retyped the code, hit enter, and 'Invalid' appeared again.

"I'm sorry, Agent Treehorn, I can't unlock my phone."

The woman's eyes teared up.

"All my memories of my mom and Luke are on this phone…"

Treehorn asked gently, "Has it ever done this before?"

"Only if I typed in the wrong numbers."

"Would you please try it one more time?" he requested.

Winter did but the phone still wouldn't allow her access.

"I can have my lab staff download the data for you."

Treehorn handed her two business cards.

"Here's my contact information. Can you write down your address, cellphone number, and its password? Please add your mom's number and password if you know it. We'll pull her records from the telephone company to see who she called for help with Father Bowden."

She wrote down the required information and handed him both mobile phones and one of the business cards; the other business card she kept in case she needed to contact him.

"You have my permission to access both of our phone's information."

Treehorn handed her a permission form he had filled out which she willingly signed. He whispered something to her.

She smiled graciously and said, "Thanks."

The agent slid the phones and business card into a plastic evidence bag. His diligent staff would do their job. No one should lose memories of their loved ones.

57

Treehorn and Winter moved to the living room and front entrance as Thomas and Melanie entered.

"Mrs. LaGrange, this is my partner, Special Agent Melanie Hopper."

"I'm so sorry for your loss," Melanie said, holding out her hand for Winter to shake.

"Thank you," Winter said. Turning to look at the second man she added, "Hello, Thomas."

"I'm sorry, Winter. It's been a rough year for you."

"For both of us."

Thomas looked at the Federal agent who wasn't a local resident.

"I'm staying here for a while. Did you get what you needed?"

Nodding, Treehorn reached his hand out to Winter and said caringly, "I want to thank you for your time. I'll be in touch."

"Please contact me if you have any further questions, Agent Treehorn."

Melanie turned to Thomas and asked, "Can you give me a lift back to my vehicle when you leave?"

The captain nodded. Treehorn squinted at Melanie.

Meeting her partner's stare, Melanie explained, "I'll stay in case anyone has information that can further assist in the investigation."

The agent shook Thomas' hand as he said, "Then I'll see both of you in the morning at the morgue."

Treehorn drove to St. Philomena's Catholic Church and parked. Opening the evidence bag, he removed the phone and business card. Then he used his own phone to dial Loveta Chilton's number. The phone in his other hand rang. He terminated the call when his number appeared on the dead woman's device.

The agent then called the FBI's communications department located in Quantico, Virginia.

"Tech Garland," a gruff, forward-speaking woman answered.

"Hi Hilda, John Treehorn."

"Great, more work!" stated a pleasantly sarcastic voice.

"Makes the day go by faster," Treehorn countered, "Until…"

"…my retirement," she said with a chuckle, "What do you need?"

"Two mobile phones. Data on the first, data and trace on the second."

The agent provided her with the setup instructions and detailed information.

"I have written permission to access both devices. I'll email it and wait for your confirmation."

"Give me a couple of minutes," Hilda replied professionally.

Treehorn scanned the written permission form and sent it to her department. While he waited, the agent checked his emails and sent one to his mother on the Navajo Indian Reservation.

"Treehorn?" Garland reconfirmed the caller.

"Yes."

"It's all set up."

"I want it pinged every fifteen minutes starting now. Put the date and time in each message when sent."

"Okay, for how long?"

"Keep pinging it until further notice. Email me if the phone changes location. I'll provide instructions at that time."

"Thanks for the work."

Treehorn responded, "I know you'll be leaving on time and the next two shifts will deal with this."

The agent didn't wait for her comment.

"I'll call LaGrange's phone right now and leave a message. Have a good evening."

Hilda chose her battles well. "You, too."

Treehorn flipped his business card over and dialed the digits on the back. It rang three times and the voicemail activated, "*Hi. You've reached Winter LaGrange. Please leave your name and number. Thanks.*"

The Fed spoke distinctly, "Hello, *Killer*. This is FBI Special Agent John Treehorn. You made a mistake."

The agent's lip curled as he tossed his phone onto the passenger seat. He then started his vehicle and drove to his lodging. Treehorn asked himself the investigative question: What was the motive for killing the priest and housekeeper?

The agent arrived at the hotel with no notification that the cellphone's location had moved. He changed into his reflective running gear and left the hotel for his nightly exercise. He knew tomorrow he would have more questions than answers. That was the job. A never-ending puzzle of crime and justice. As his feet pounded the pavement he knew one thing: the church wouldn't surrender any secrets, in the name of their God.

Treehorn telephoned Samantha after he'd returned to the hotel and showered. His call went to her voicemail.

"Sam. Let's talk. I have more to explain. Give us a chance."

He stared out at the darkness and waited for a response from her. None arrived.

The agent's telephone beeped. He opened his email from Quantico.

"The telephone has changed location. Second location is now fixed. Please advise. —Technician Carol Lee."

Treehorn replied, "Continue with same instructions for the night."

The dark dressed man came out of the shadows. His leather-gloved hand opened the blue mailbox flap, while the other deposited four tiny postage paid packages into its depths. Then, he disappeared back into the night.

Chapter Five

Professional Courtesy

The morning security staff greeted Treehorn as he signed the log before entering the locked wing of the Clinton County Morgue. The lingering smell of death and chemicals caused the bile to rise in his throat. He unwrapped a cinnamon candy to cover the taste.

Dr. Elliot Spencer leaned against one of the refrigerated compartments that made up one wall. Thomas and Melanie listened to the man finish a joke's punchline:

"Nobody puts a baby in a coroner."

All three of them roared with laughter.

"I'll have to remember that one!" Melanie chuckled.

Spotting the Fed, the coroner greeted him, "Good Morning, Agent Treehorn."

"Good morning."

"There's coffee in my office."

"No thanks."

"Thought you'd have a stronger stomach," Thomas made his early patronizing jab.

Treehorn's telephone pinged which prevented his reply. He examined the early message.

63

"Cellphone is on the move. Will keep tracking. Please advise of any change."

Treehorn returned his device to his pocket without replying to Thomas.

Melanie handed Treehorn two medical reports and whispered, "Did you get any sleep?"

Treehorn leaned into her space and replied, "Do me a *favor*, do your job."

Melanie frowned and stepped away from her partner.

Dr. Spencer walked to an X-ray viewer and flicked the switch.

"Father Howard Bowden, seventy years of age. The gun of choice, a .40 caliber. Single shot to the head. He experienced TIAs (transient ischemic attacks), also commonly known as mini strokes."

Thomas added, "Living on borrowed time."

"He had a good time, too," the coroner joked.

The three LEOs waited for the punchline, "His blood work tested positive for syphilis. Based on statements I've gathered, it was probably in its tertiary stage. Neurosyphilis causes a variety of psychiatric symptoms: mania, depression, dementia, and psychosis."

Melanie's facial expression showed humor hearing the report.

Treehorn's didn't.

"Could syphilis have caused the recent erratic behavior observed by his congregation?"

Dr. Spencer nodded.

"Yes, but not relevant. He would have died from a stroke within weeks from the damage noted. The removal of his ear, eye, and tongue were all postmortem as was the stab wound."

"Anything else?"

"No, that's it for the priest."

He removed the X-rays and replaced them with the woman's.

"Loveta Chilton, sixty. Cause of death, a single .40 caliber gunshot to the head. She had hypertension, type II diabetes, weight-controlled. One live birth. No other health issues. She's listed as a widow."

"Was she tested for syphilis?" Melanie asked before Treehorn.

"Of course. It was negative."

"Anything else?" Thomas questioned.

"I sent both bullets to ballistics. I read your preliminary report and it stated the gun had been fired three times. No other bullet or lead fragments were found in either victim."

The coroner looked at Thomas, commenting, "It's good to see your return, sir."

"I'll let you know when it feels like that."

He understood the man's struggle.

"Jimmy called from your station. He has some results for you."

"Thanks, Doc."

"Sorry I couldn't offer more in this investigation."

Treehorn shook the coroner's hand. "Thanks for your help."

The three LEOs walked out of the morgue with their reports in hand.

"I'll meet you at my precinct," Thomas said, walking toward his vehicle.

Melanie's curiosity prevailed, "Why were you gone?"

Thomas avoided her gaze as he replied, "I took a personal leave of absence."

Treehorn's eyes met Melanie's, but neither commented.

The three LEOs met outside the station's forensic laboratory. Thomas swiped his security badge and the door electronically opened. The two agents followed and naturally checked out their surroundings.

Thomas shouted, "Jimmy!"

Surprised, a pale young man jumped out from behind his computer.

"Mysteries, Jimmy."

"Revelations, Captain."

The pair chuckled and shook hands.

"The place hasn't been the same without you!"

"Jimmy Cromwell, FBI Special Agents John Treehorn and Melanie Hopper. They've been assigned to Father Bowden's case. I have Loveta Chilton'."

The late-twenties lab tech glanced at Thomas and then the Feds.

"How're you doing?" he sniffed.

"Acclimating to the area," Treehorn responded as he watched the nervous, young man.

"So, what do we have, J?"

A red-taped evidence box sat open on the table. Beside it, the wooden-handled gun and knife lay secured in their own boxes, as well as two bullets and a page filled with plastic evidence bags. All had CSU chain-of-custody signatures.

"Primary items," Treehorn emphasized.

Jimmy held up an antique gold knife stained with blood.

"This was used to remove the body parts of the priest. Then, stabbed to his chest. It's owned by the church. Two sets of fingerprints were found on it. those of Father Bowden and Loveta Chilton. I sent blood samples out for DNA testing. Questions?"

Thomas and Melanie uttered, "No."

Jimmy glanced at Treehorn who shook his head once.

The lab tech held up the next item. The torn page, blood-stained, that had been stabbed to Father Bowden's chest.

"The fingerprints on it and the handwriting matched the priest's. We're pulling the pressed imprint lettering off the page's front and back."

The three LEOs listened intently.

"It's the top half of a page from a bound journal. We narrowed it down to a local manufacturer. It wasn't an uncommon item."

Jimmy's job history contained many notable stories but this scored high on his list.

"It was a diary of illicit confessions. Perverted, huh?"

Considering the broader ramifications, Treehorn asked, "Have you kept this information within the confines of this department?"

"Yes, sir. I've secured the testing and their results."

Melanie added, "That's a good idea because when the church hears about it, they'll interfere in this investigation."

Everyone was on the same page about that.

Lifting the box containing the gun, Jimmy clarified, "This was the murder weapon of both the priest and Mrs. Chilton."

"Appropriate conclusion, Jimmy."

"I've sent some DNA samples to trace, too."

The three LEOs watched as Jimmy broke out into a sweat and avoided eye contact.

Jimmy lifted the bags that contained the two bullets.

"Ballistics also matched this gun to another crime."

The tech's hand shook.

The captain leaned forward and asked, "What crime?"

Treehorn watched the men's interaction.

Sweat appeared on Jimmy's forehead as he blurted out, "Last year, your case."

Thomas didn't see what was in front of him…but what was in his past.

"The suicide…"

Janet Riley Foster Home, one year ago

Captain Thomas Brooks passed under the yellow police tape that surrounded the children's home. All of its inhabitants had been immediately removed to a safe environment. The trooper signed in and covered his black leather shoes with the crime scene foot booties. He walked down the hallway where red tape marked the teenager's door.

Inside Cate Dixon's corpse lay sprawled on the twin bed. The cause of death, a single gunshot wound to her head. A trail of blood had trickled down and dried from her temple into her hair. On her neck was a dainty, gold cross.

The curtain billowed from the night breeze as if waving toward the mirror on the wall, where three words were written in red lipstick: "I WAS RAPED!"

The faces and voices flashed in Thomas' nightmares:

CSU Harris: "The weapon's missing, sir."

Dr. Eliot Spencer: "I ruled her death a suicide."

Jimmy: "Your DNA."

And finally, Major Morgan's sympathetic face as he broke the news: "She was your child, your daughter."

Thomas returned to the present when Jimmy finished his sentence, "...Cate Dixon, your daughter."

Melanie gasped audibly as she placed her hand on his arm. "I'm so sorry."

"You're officially off these cases," Treehorn stated the bitter fact. Thomas didn't want to hear him.

"Your daughter's case will be reopened, sir," Jimmy said, voicing the obvious.

"It was never closed," Thomas said sadly as he turned and walked out.

Melanie glanced at her colleague.

"I'll pull her investigation."

The lab's phone rang as Treehorn invaded Melanie's space, "Don't bother. I pulled her file last night and read the complete case. What were you doing?"

Melanie's face flushed.

"Not all of us live and breathe the job, *partner*."

Treehorn's lip curled in disgust. He turned and walked away without commenting.

Jimmy eyed the last standing agent, "Could you tell the captain that Major Morgan is waiting for him in his office?"

Treehorn found Thomas outside of the lab. Two men who had suffered the loss of a loved one.

The captain held a delicate gold cross and chain between his fingers.

"I made a promise to her when I learned that she was my daughter. I told her spirit I would find him even if I had to go to hell and back."

Thomas rubbed the cross and then dropped it into his pocket.

"I know pain," Treehorn sympathized.

Thomas met the agent's weary eyes as he responded, "Who?"

"My wife was murdered." Treehorn didn't add that she died in front of him or that he relived the painful memory daily.

"Did you question your God that day?"

"No, because the Great Spirit didn't use his hands to beat her to death."

"Tragedy alters the path of one's life."

"Yes, but I wouldn't be standing here today as an FBI agent if it hadn't occurred. The one thing I don't regret is my time with Skyler."

"You're lucky. I never had the opportunity to meet my daughter."

"Then, help me find the man who assaulted her," Treehorn offered a compromise.

Thomas shook his head.

"I'm off the case, you said so yourself."

"Do either of us follow orders?" Treehorn raised his stitched brow.

Locating the men in the hallway Melanie said, "Thomas, your boss needs you in your office."

The captain acknowledged it with a brief nod.

"I'll introduce you both and we can inform him of the change in the investigation."

The three LEOs walked to the administrative section of the building passing the investigative unit.

Treehorn observed the staff working diligently, including the two State Police from the church.

Captain Brooks' administrative assistant, a woman in her mid-fifties, watched her boss arrive. Her pale face pinched in distress.

Thomas pressed the button on his pocketed cellphone.

"Wait here," the woman relayed the order to the three as she answered her ringing telephone, "Captain Brooks' office. Stella Hunter speaking."

73

Thomas walked past the woman as he spoke into his device, "It's my office."

The agents watched as the woman slammed down her handset and the man entered his own office without knocking.

The Feds stopped at the woman's desk and presented their identification.

"FBI Special Agents John Treehorn and Melanie Hopper. I'm the lead investigator assigned to Father Bowden's murder."

He handed her his business card which she thankfully accepted.

"Good luck working with that evil man. You better go into the meeting since it's related to your case."

"Thank you."

Treehorn and Melanie entered the office where three strangers sat.

A New York State Police officer dressed in a high-ranking grey uniform with a single gold oak leaf pinned to his shoulder, representing his rank of Major, rose from the chair behind the desk and shook the agents' hands.

"Major Steven Morgan."

"FBI Special Agents John Treehorn and Melanie Hopper."

Thomas leaned casually against a side wall. A deceptive pose, Treehorn noted, as Melanie closed the wooden door.

"Captain Thomas Brooks for the record."

He glanced at Treehorn and then at the two men who sat in the chairs in front of his desk.

The major conducted the introductions, "Father William Wilkens and the Archdiocese Attorney Aaron Robbins."

Treehorn sized up the two well-dressed men. The first, the thirty-year-old priest, dressed in a black suit with its standard white collar, stood and nodded to the agents. He then returned to his seat. The second, a fifty-year-old white man, wore his thousand-dollar suit well on his legal shoulders. The expensive leather briefcase wasn't necessary to identify him as a lawyer.

The man glanced once at the FBI agents, made no effort to acknowledge them, and then intentionally ignored the two.

Melanie watched Treehorn's face show contempt for the man's insolence while Thomas' simply smirked. It was as if the captain knew the agent held the upper hand.

The major sat down without commenting.

Treehorn intentionally moved and stood behind the lawyer as the meeting commenced.

Robbins spoke first, "I've been assigned to represent St. Philomena's Catholic Church. We've been told that a page from a diary was found on Father Bowden's body."

"Who told you that?" Thomas demanded.

He wanted them identified.

"Did you recover a diary page? Yes or no?" the lawyer demanded.

"Tell me who told you, then I'll provide an answer," the captain parried.

"Stop!" Major Morgan issued the response.

Thomas glanced at his boss, who nodded.

"The blood was still wet on it."

"A written confession found on a priest's body is still the property of the Church. We want it returned immediately."

Treehorn answered, "No!"

Father Wilkens added, "You can't convict a single soul with the information gathered from it. I'm an attorney, too."

"Must come in handy in your line of work," Thomas cracked.

"Major!" Robbins' face flushed.

Pointing a finger at the priest Thomas snapped, "Your predecessor was murdered! What's more of a priority? Catching his killer or hiding the fact that your man of the cloth kept an illicit diary of confessions?"

The major stated the obvious: "He should have taken it with him to his grave."

Father Wilkens furthered, "It was a misjudgment on his part to write down secrets."

Attorney Robbins and the priest stood.

Father Wilkens gave his opinion to the State Police Major, "The page is the property of the Church."

Captain Brooks countered, "The page is the property of the State."

"The page is the property of the FBI and I'm a lawyer, too," Treehorn clarified, stating his own legal background for the record.

Lawyers Robbins and Wilkens turned to face the Special Agent.

Treehorn stared them both down.

"Let's take it to a federal judge where it will become a permanent public record. I'll guarantee it will hit the news before my courtroom appearance, even with an injunction."

"You wouldn't!" Robbins stammered, eyeing the agent's bruised face and knuckles.

Father Wilkens saw the black and blue contusions. He wondered how the other man had fared in the apparent fistfight.

Treehorn's stitched eyebrow rose as he leaned toward the men in an aggressive stance.

Melanie bobbed her head once for the church attorney and then once for the lawyer-turned-priest.

Catching on to Melanie's flippant nods as he watched Treehorn stand his ground, Thomas added, "I think we should release it to the public just for the *fun* of it."

Attorney Robbins resigned himself to the inevitable. "No, of course not."

"So, we're in agreement?" Major Morgan asked, but made it an order, "No one's releasing the page, or even that it exists. I'll send a memo out—ordering my staff not to release any details of these investigations."

Thomas asked, "Who told you we had the page in the first place? I'm making that a condition."

Major Morgan supported his man by staying silent.

Attorney Robbins hesitated before answering, "We have a confidential hotline to report..."

"Crimes," Thomas filled in the blank.

"...infractions," the priest clarified.

"I'd like to hear the message and when you received it," Treehorn requested.

"It's a confidential hotline to a church. What part do you not understand, Agent Treehorn?" the church attorney voiced his legal authority.

"Do either of you know why Father Bowden or Loveta Chilton were murdered?" The agent grilled the pair.

Robbins avoided Treehorn's eyes as he reached for his briefcase.

Father Wilkens held out his hand to the Fed.

"If I can help you in any way within the confines of my position, I will do so."

Treehorn shook his hand and gave him his business card.

"The page is evidence in a murder. It's the reason I have it."

Diplomacy works, sometimes.

Major Morgan issued his directive, "We'll keep it quiet. I suggest you do the same."

Aaron Robbins and Father Wilkens looked at each other. They lost the fight of taking possession of Father Bowden's written page. Now, one hoped while the other prayed that the Feds and the State Police kept the diary information classified.

Major Morgan ended the meeting. "If there's nothing else: Good day, gentlemen."

Melanie opened the door for the pair's departure and closed it after they walked past.

Thomas and Treehorn's eyes met. Silently communicating the small win.

The major looked at the agents as he returned to his chair.

"Have a seat. Why in God's name would a priest keep a diary?"

Thomas chuckled, "Wait until they find out the diary's missing."

Morgan snorted and shook his head, "Agent Treehorn, Hopper. Ever deal with a case like this?"

"No, I can't say that we have." Focusing on this case, he added, "Did your ballistics staff update you on the new development?"

"Yes, Jimmy emailed me the updates," The major replied, "I'm sorry, Thomas, I'll have to remove you from the case."

Treehorn added a request, "I'd like Captain Brooks to remain as a liaison between my agency and yours. It'll keep him in the loop as a professional courtesy."

The Supervisor glanced at Thomas, wondering whether he thought the FBI agent had a hidden agenda, "As long as someone goes to jail."

Treehorn nodded once to major.

Morgan pressed the intercom to Stella's desk, "Send them in."

Two familiar faces entered in uniforms.

"Have you two agents been introduced to Troopers Rita Holmes and Doug Milner?"

Rita answered for both, "Agent Treehorn," Doug said, nodding.

Treehorn introduced his partner, "Special Agent Melanie Hopper."

Major Morgan continued, "The Feds have Father Bowden's investigation. I'm assigning you two to Loveta Chilton's murder and Cate Dixon's rape and suicide. Agent Treehorn, they'll be under your supervision. We know the gun connects all of these cases. Find out who owns it."

Treehorn nodded once before asking, "Are we done?"

Major Morgan shook Treehorn's hand.

"I'm heading back to Albany today. The captain will provide me with updates and contact me if necessary."

Treehorn understood. He wasn't to bother the man and that suited him just fine.

Thomas closed the door after the Feds' departure. The State Police meeting wasn't over.

Major Morgan eyed his colleague explaining. "Thomas, you'll need to pass your firearms certification for full reinstatement."

"Understood."

The high-ranking Supervisor continued, "What I tell you stays in this room. Agreed?"

The three New York State Police officers—two troopers and a captain—nodded.

"You two are in charge, *on paper*, but Thomas is silently in charge of his daughter's investigation. You two will receive credit in the end."

"Yes, sir."

The two officers understood the power of authority.

Thomas gave them their first directive, "Pull Cate's files and evidence boxes. Take them to the conference room. Treehorn's smart, and from what his director says, the agent won't stop until justice is served. What's our motto?"

Trooper Rita Holmes answered, "Excellence through knowledge."

"Exactly. Let him work these cases because we want justice, too."

As the two Feds entered their assigned workspace, Treehorn's telephone pinged. He glanced at Hilda from Quantico's message: *"Your device - now located in Albany. Please advise."*

He typed a reply, *"No further tracking needed. Thank you. —Treehorn."*

Then he typed a quick message to his administrative assistant in DC: *"Hi, Abby, please secure a small package that will be arriving soon. —Treehorn."*

He lifted his lips in a smile as he thought of his dedicated office staff.

Melanie's ongoing curiosity, that she now nicknamed 'Treehorn's Mysteries', motivated her to ask, "New girlfriend?"

His smile disappeared and his eyes bored into her. Silent and furious.

The hairs on the back of her neck rose and she waited for her due punishment.

Instead, Treehorn issued a single instruction, "Find out who made the call to the church's hotline."

"The Church won't surrender that information."

Treehorn gritted his teeth, "Are you going to question every order I give?"

"If they don't make sense."

"I think the killer called and he's playing games with the church."

"The State Police are smart. They should have caught that but I'll get right on it since you asked nicely."

"Like I've said, *do your job*."

Melanie understood the power of seniority.

Treehorn made a quick purchase on his cellphone for overnight delivery to his office and then sent instructions for Abby to take care of it when it arrived. A device that will catch a criminal in action.

Chapter Six

Town Folk

Thomas eyed his two troopers as he said, "Let's get to work. I'll recommend a promotion when someone is arrested."

The officers knew this case wasn't about dangling a carrot in front of them. It was their supervisor's personal pursuit and agenda.

The three members of the New York State Police entered the conference room. Ahead, Agents Treehorn and Hopper had posted the information from the investigation onto a single bulletin board. A second stood off to the side of the room.

"I made a fresh pot of coffee," Melanie informed the LEOs, handing Thomas a cup.

Treehorn noticed she didn't ask him how he took his drink.

Thomas whispered to Melanie, "He's not much of a talker is he? What's his history?"

"Not open for discussion. But he does have one of the highest closure rates in the FBI for a lead investigator."

Thomas wasn't surprised. He knew why his friend, FBI Director Andrew Mason, sent the man.

"Let's get to work!" Treehorn ordered the group.

Thomas wheeled the other board from its corner and swung it around. It was completely covered with Cate Dixon's rape and suicide crime scene photos, ballistic reports, and DNA results.

Treehorn took a hard look at it, then joined the others as they worked diligently to cover the second board with all of the Father Bowden and Loveta Chilton's investigative files.

The garbage can slowly filled with food containers and coffee cups as time passed.

After several hours, Troopers Holmes and Milner left the room with Melanie to take a break.

As Treehorn examined Cate Dixon's bulletin board, he asked the obvious.

"Why was your daughter in foster care?" The Fed didn't pull any punches.

"Her mother, Tina, left the state when our relationship ended and never informed me she was pregnant. They were returning to the area when she was killed in a car accident north of Keeseville. Car registration and her license listed her surname from Texas. No connections to New York."

"No legal notification?"

"Tina had married. I wasn't a contact and my name wasn't listed as the father on Cate's birth certificate. My daughter was given her stepfather's surname."

"Why didn't the man protect her?"

"When my staff finally tracked him down in New Mexico, he told the investigator the kid wasn't his and he wasn't legally responsible for her. He never filed adoption papers. Mr. Dixon then informed him that his soon-to-be-ex-wife had packed her and her kid's bags one day while he was at work. When he arrived home, he found a note informing him she had filed divorce papers and he would be served. The kid had no one."

"Department of Social Services took guardianship?"

Thomas nodded and continued, "Cate entered the foster care system where she was sexually abused and committed suicide."

"When did you realize it?" Treehorn asked.

"What? That I was conducting an investigation on my own daughter? The lab cross-referenced all the personnel at the crime scene."

"The standard exclusion policy to rule out contamination."

"Exactly! I was flagged. My DNA was retested and the results showed that I was her biological father."

"Then, you were removed from the case?"

Thomas nodded.

"And ordered to see a psychiatrist. I took a leave of absence when no new leads developed."

He pointed to the two men and one woman's images posted on Cate's bulletin board.

"Who are they?" Treehorn asked, looking at the three white individuals.

"The so-called pillars of this community. They recognize the criminals in this town."

"*Knowing about* and *participating in* crimes are two different things," Treehorn reminded him.

Thomas pointed to the first photo of a greasy white male with black, unkempt hair wearing a dirty white cook's apron over his potbelly.

"Granger, diner owner."

Treehorn examined his image as he read: *'Joseph Granger, 35'.*

The man's black eyes appeared void of all emotion.

Thomas moved to the next picture.

"Myers, town historian."

The agent observed: *'Gardenia Myers, sixty'*, a small, sickly, pale-faced, red headed female with beady blue eyes.

"Lastly the town judge, Stiles. Well, let me rephrase that—*incompetent* town judge."

Treehorn examined the third photograph as he read: *'Dooley Stiles, sixty'*. A white, obese, grey-bearded man with closely spaced cruel eyes.

"In small towns, Agent Treehorn, everybody knows everybody's business."

Thomas pointed to Father Bowden's image—dressed in his black suit with its white collar. He knew everything about the crime too."

"Yes, he did, but how do we use it to convict the criminal?"

"The priest spoke from the grave. He left us two clues."

Thomas pointed to the crime scene photograph of the antique revolver.

Treehorn spoke the fact, "The gun ties these cases together."

"True. The problem: there's no recorded owner or serial number. The gun was manufactured prior to the Gun Control Act of 1968."

"Which required guns to have serial numbers."

"Exactly. We do know the weapon was manufactured in Europe."

"The second clue?"

"Pillars of the community, sinners of the community. We have a diary."

"No, we have a page *from* a diary."

"Yes, but they don't know that."

"Are the DNA results back from Father Bowden?"

Thomas dialed the lab and handed the telephone handset to Treehorn. "Your case."

The agent raised his eyebrow and hit the speaker button on the phone. "Jimmy, Special Agent Treehorn. Any update on the results of the priest's DNA?"

The lab tech replied, "Sometime tomorrow."

"Thank you."

Treehorn terminated the call and then went to the board to examine Father Bowden's post-mortem head injuries.

"What would motivate someone to cut the priest post-mortem?"

"Did someone hear an evil, see an evil, and speak of an evil?" Thomas explained, pointing to the images of the small town's citizens. "The priest's telephone call. He said, 'I did a terrible thing, I lied for you once—never again!'"

"Was that the killer who called?"

"Or, did it have nothing to do with the case?"

"He lied for someone and the housekeeper stated it upset him."

"One of them?"

"We don't know."

"Unless they did and they're not telling."

"Why protect a dead man?"

"Who said they're protecting him?"

Melanie and the pair of troopers returned carrying sandwiches and drinks.

Treehorn ordered his partner, "Pull the phone records of the church and rectory. The church will attempt to block it, but I'll deal with it in court if that happens."

Thomas pointed to the bulletin boards now covered with documentation and images.

"Holmes and Milner, I want you to re-examine these two displays. A fresh perspective since neither of you worked Cate's case. The gun connects these two investigations. Somewhere here, there has to be a clue that could identify a rapist and a killer."

Melanie examined the image of the wooden-handled revolver, "I'll take the weapon."

She knew her Alcohol, Tobacco, and Firearms background could be helpful in deciphering its origins.

Thomas saw Melanie's focus on the gun.

"My daughter wasn't alone when she died. The foster home caretaker ran to the room as soon as she heard the gunshot. Whoever was in that room grabbed the weapon and slipped out the window. I've asked myself numerous times, *Why take the weapon?*"

"Was there any clue as to how she came to have the gun?"

"Dead end. Not a single person knew she had it."

Melanie stated her opinion, "What if she had it for protection? The interview with the pharmacist revealed that she purchased the pregnancy test just prior to using it. What if she told someone about the abuse and they gave her the gun to kill her abuser, but once she found out she was pregnant she killed herself instead?"

Treehorn listened to the theory.

"Then there would have been three hands besides hers that touched the gun. The person who gave it to her, the individual who removed it after the suicide, and then the killer who committed the two murders."

92

Melanie countered, "Was the abuser and shooter the same person? I'll research the gun with the ATF database." Leaning into Treehorn's personal space, she whispered, "You seem a little preoccupied. Something bothering you?"

Treehorn glanced once at his partner.

"This town feels like a cesspool of deviant behavior. Like a cloak of immorality is the norm. I get the sense that everyone holds a piece to this puzzle except us."

Melanie smirked. "That's really deep, Treehorn. Would it have helped if you interviewed the town folk?"

Treehorn clenched his jaw.

"How's that phone record coming along?"

Melanie flushed. "They're not releasing it without a warrant which they know you won't obtain."

Treehorn wasn't finished yet, "Shady sent me a message on Monday. Something about a favor?"

Melanie frowned as she returned to her work without commenting.

Two investigators from the New York State Police Bureau of Criminal Investigation, Ryan and Barney, entered the conference room with files in their hands.

Thomas pointed to Treehorn.

"The Feds now are leading both murder investigations. Troopers Milner and Holmes are in charge of Cate Dixon's case. The ballistics came back on the .40 caliber revolver. All three individuals died by the same gun, so I've been removed from the case."

Treehorn eyed the two suit-and-tie professional men. Someone would take them for federal agents if they stood in the lobby of the J. Edgar Hoover Building.

"What did you find?"

BCI Ryan started, "We interviewed the so-called pillars of the community and canvased the square."

"What are their names?" Treehorn asked to verify their identities.

Thomas interrupted, "Let me guess: Joseph Granger, diner owner; Gardenia Myers, town historian; and Dooley Stiles, town judge."

The two officers nodded.

BCI Barney asked, "Small-town guess?"

Thomas glanced at Treehorn as he explained, "I worked this case for months and those names kept appearing. What did you find?"

Ryan read their reports. "Joseph Granger was asleep at home at the time of the murders. He told us he didn't know anything and to stop bothering him. He went real quiet, stunned, when we told him Father Bowden had been murdered. He then slammed the door without commenting."

Thomas remembered one day he observed the short, swarthy man at the Altona Diner.

Joseph Granger—a short, greasy man with a pock-marked face and beady black eyes—watched the waitress work his small-town diner as a few patrons ate his cheap meals. He visited with the customers and every time the young waitress would pass him, he slapped her on the buttocks. She grimaced but kept her mouth shut so she could remain gainfully employed in the crappy establishment.

Thomas remembered paying his bill, coming up behind Granger, snapping his arm behind his back, and slamming his face into a customer's French fries. Then he whispered, "You touch another woman, ever, within my sight and I'll haul your ass off to jail. Do I make myself clear?" The greasy potatoes in gravy moved on the customer's plate as Joseph nodded.

"He's liked by some and despised by others. The diner's a hotbed of gossip and lies. The night of Cate's suicide Joseph Granger and Father Bowden alibied that they were at the diner drinking coffee. They stated in their police interviews that they heard the shot but didn't see anyone approach the diner."

Investigator Barney read from his report, "Town historian Gardenia Myers stated she and her husband were asleep at home. After she blurted that out, she slammed the door in my face."

Thomas remembered meeting Gardenia Myers the same day at the small-town diner. She sat quietly in her very expensive outfit that clearly didn't fit the greasy spoon establishment. Her pale fingers held a china teacup and, from the way she presented herself, you could tell she believed she was better than everyone else.

Thomas added, "The woman rewrites the town's history to suit her agenda. She denied seeing anything the evening Cate died even though she takes a walk at the same time every night. Gardenia is the resident sneak and backstabber, but everyone is too ignorant to see the truth. I've watched her manipulate them like a marionette for years."

Ryan finished with the last person, "Judge Dooley Stiles said he was at the town hall arraigning a DWI. That was verified by the patrol officer. Dooley stated he had no further information and then he slammed his door."

Treehorn watched Thomas' face flush with anger as he recalled, "I remember seeing him one day at the diner as he shoveled food into his filthy bearded face. His battered wife sat across from him, her bruised face lowered in shame."

Thomas' eyes met Treehorn's. The pair understood.

"The esteemed judge was home beating his wife the night of Cate's suicide. Mrs. Stiles was admitted to the women's shelter where she checked herself out the next morning."

Investigator Barney jested, "These are the pillars of our society?"

"For the weak-minded here? Yes," Thomas replied bitterly.

Treehorn stayed silent and glanced at his partner's work.

"It's reported that they cooperated with DNA testing," Melanie read the document.

"All of the men volunteered samples to prove their innocence. Not a single match. I sensed they hid something."

"Did the priest provide a DNA sample?" Treehorn asked.

The LEOs searched the documents to determine whether the man had been tested or the results.

"We can't locate any."

Thomas stated, "Jimmy will have the priest's DNA tomorrow. That will answer our question."

Examining the bulletin boards, Treehorn suggested, "Let's call it a night, team."

Thomas pulled his vehicle into the *Gateway Medical Facility* parking lot of for his mandatory counseling. He entered the minimalist office building, dressed in full uniform.

The simple plaque labeled its entrance, *'Dr. Mario Mancini, Clinical & Forensic Psychiatrist.'*

A female receptionist in her mid-thirties sat behind a desk with headphones listening to a recording, while she typed the medical notes on a computer. She lifted one ear jack upon seeing Thomas and said cheerfully, "You can go right in."

"Thanks, Marjorie."

Thomas walked down the carpeted hallway and knocked twice on the door. Professional courtesy.

"Come in."

Dr. Mario Mancini, a fifty-year-old, dark-haired, very well-dressed man sat behind an expensive, obsessively organized desk. Numerous diplomas and achievements lined his wall. The psychiatrist examined, over his bifocals, his highly punctual patient.

"Nice uniform."

Thomas smirked and casually crossed his leg to get comfortable in the leather chair..

Dr. Mancini examined the awards pinned to the breast area of the grey uniform.

"I returned to work."

"I can see that. Nice pin cushion."

"I earned each one."

"Never doubted that. What made you finally return?"

"A case. I'm sure you've heard about it on the radio since Monday morning."

"Father Bowden's or your daughter's?"

"Actually, neither. I was assigned to another investigation but a conflict arose. Now, I'm an official bystander behind an FBI Special Agent and two State Policemen."

"What about Cate's case?"

"Did I mention the State Police?" Thomas questioned, eyebrow raised.

"Why did you come here?"

Thomas took a long look at the intuitive doctor who had more degrees on his wall than he would ever use.

"My boss ordered me to. I think he suspects I'm crazy and thinks you give me perspective."

"Mentally ill? No. Manipulative? Yes. Perspective on what exactly? You were only a sperm donor."

"See, perspective."

"You were never a father."

Thomas didn't argue the point.

"What's more important to you, continuing with this delusion that you were a parent or realistically being a cop?"

Thomas examined his clean-clipped fingernails as he said, sadly, "She left me without telling me she carried our child in her belly."

"Yes, she did. Rinse, repeat."

"Will I ever lose the anger?"

"Probably not."

Dr. Mancini believed in cold, hard facts and cynical conclusions.

"But then, you can't lose something you never truly had."

"Doing my job," Thomas answered the man's prior question. Then, he abruptly stood and walked out into the cold, rainy night.

The man's behavior made Dr. Mancini frown. He knew the captain would return because his boss ordered him to do so.

Thomas sat in front of his fire sipping a liqueur when his cellphone rang. He glanced at its caller id.

"I knew you would call after I messaged you."

The deep man's voice asked, "Did you make a mistake?"

"I underestimated."

"Can it be corrected?"

"Yes."

The wall clock cuckooed.

Thomas threw his glass into the fire and watched as it exploded.

Treehorn received an encrypted message from Raven.

"Do you miss the Land of your People?"

The agent walked to the hotel lobby and pulled out a prepaid credit card from his wallet. He used it on the landline to call his Navajo partner's burner phone on the Rez. "Hello my friend. What did you find?"

"Tina Dixon created an elaborate fake identification. Driver's license, social security, everything—including a forged birth certificate for Cate so there would be no problem with school enrollment."

"Why?"

"Because someone with a federal security clearance searched for her."

"Who?"

"Someone above our paygrade."

Chapter Seven

Lie and Wait

The windshield wipers struggled against the driving rain as Treehorn drove to the police station. As he drove, the agent reflected on the words of Father Wilkens in Major Morgan's office. *'It was a misjudgment to write down one's secrets.'* Although, Treehorn suspected the church knew about Father Bowden's behavior.

When he arrived, the precinct was full of uniformed officers, plain-clothed investigators, and administrative staff. Many of the officers openly stared at the Special Agent. Treehorn sensed ominous news had been dispensed prior to his arrival.

Melanie, Jimmy, and Troopers Milner and Holmes awaited them.

Treehorn eyed the group.

"What's happened?"

Thomas entered behind the Fed before anyone spoke.

Lightning struck nearby and the room lights flickered as the two men removed their drenched overcoats.

"What happened?" Treehorn demanded.

Jimmy handed the Fed the document while avoiding Thomas' gaze.

"Here are the DNA results of Father Bowden."

Melanie's eyes met Thomas' as she said, "It's disturbing news."

The captain snapped. "I've gathered that from how everyone's eyes are avoiding me. What is it, Jimmy?"

"I cross-referenced Father Bowden's DNA to your daughter's case because of the ballistics."

Melanie added, "It's a break in the case."

"I promise not to kill the messenger," Thomas offered.

Treehorn answered, "The priest and your daughter's fetus have matching genetic markers."

Thomas' hand shook slightly as he accepted the paper from the agent.

"Was he the rapist?"

Jimmy replied, "No."

Treehorn supplemented, "The priest had a son."

Jimmy moved hastily toward the exit and said, "I'll be in the lab."

Melanie eyed her partner.

"I'll search for the record."

Handing Treehorn the results Thomas said, "The Church knew."

He grabbed a dry trench coat from the rack and walked out of the conference room.

Melanie caught up with him at the front entrance. "Where are you going?"

"To see a priest about a confession," Thomas replied, angrily shoving the door open.

Melanie watched as he jogged to his vehicle through the downpour. His trench coat flapped in the wind like a fallen angel with black wings.

Thomas sped down the wet road with his lights and siren on to part the traffic in his haste. His police SUV squealed to a halt in front of St. Philomena's Catholic Church rectory. No one answered as he pounded on the front door. Striding into the church he heard *Amazing Grace.* Then he threw his wet trench coat on the pew before starting his search for Father Wilkens.

The captain passed a carpenter as he worked on the first of two new confessional booths. The door made a unique, hollowed sound as the tradesman opened and closed it to make sure it fit perfectly in its frame.

An electrician finished adjusting the last screw in the doorbell before he tested it. The ringing reverberated throughout the holy space. The man smiled in self-appreciation for a job well done.

Thomas asked, "Do you know we call that the Devil's Doorbell?"

The smile disappeared off the worker's face as if evil truly did stand in front of him and waited to ring the bell.

Thomas passed both laborers to search the rear rooms. He tried a couple doors but they were locked.

Mrs. Lorna MacDonald, a short, thin woman near his age, blocked the hallway.

"Father Wilkens isn't seeing anyone today."

Thomas pushed her aside with one hand as he stressed, "He'll see me on official business!"

The captain opened the door beneath which a sliver of light shone.

Father Wilkens wore a white frock as he read beneath a single lamp. The whole room gave the picture of peacefulness.

Thomas knew that was an illusion as rain pelted the window.

Mrs. MacDonald stood in the doorway, neither entering nor departing.

Thomas raised his voice to be heard. "Get rid of her!"

"Thank you, Mrs. MacDonald. I'll call you when needed."

The woman glared at Thomas as she closed the door.

Father Wilkens stood and gently placed his religious history book on the table. His white gown shimmered in the lamplight.

"I'll walk you out. Now's not a good time for a visit."

Thomas clenched his fist.

"I answered my calling."

He punched the priest in the face.

The man landed back in his chair as blood gushed from his nose and splattered down his pristine clothing. He grabbed several tissues and attempted to stop its bloody flow.

Thomas casually looked around the room at the gold antiques.

Father Wilkens glared at him but remained silent.

The captain checked for dust on the vintage piece.

"I investigated a burglary here over a year ago. It was then I was introduced to your level of greed."

The priest reached for more tissues to stem the flow, allowing his assailant to ramble on.

"I caught the little thief but I didn't arrest him. His mother had given all of her money to the church and he was hungry."

"I'm sorry to hear he committed a crime."

Thomas walked to the mini refrigerator and removed an ice tray. He dumped the cubes on the white cloth that lay beneath the candlestick that he knocked aside. Then he wrapped it up and handed it to Father Wilkens.

"She was the one who committed a crime for letting her son go hungry. The kid's aunt was Betty Luzer—the rectory's old housekeeper who Sarah Sawyer replaced."

"Is there a point to this conversation?"

"When did you discover Howard Bowden had fathered a son?"

"You know I won't break Canon Law by discussing any confession, regardless of what was confided to us."

Thomas sat and appeared relaxed in a chair opposite Father Wilkens.

"You already did. Quote, *"It was a misjudgment on his part to write down one's secrets."* You weren't talking about someone else's at that time. You were talking about his own. He wrote in his diary that he had impregnated someone. Someone read it. Did they notify the Archdiocese when it happened, or did he just confess to it and the Church kept the transgression silent?"

Father Wilkens stated, "It was a misjudgment on my part to discuss it. Somehow, I think you already knew that."

Thomas grilled, "What did the priest confess? He's dead. What's it matter now?"

"The sacramental seal is unbreakable even when the penitent is dead."

Thomas smiled at the priest but emotion didn't reach his cold stare.

"It's okay. People confess to me all the time."

Father Wilkens didn't respond to the inappropriate banter as he treated his injury that had finally stopped bleeding.

"I could never understand this confession thing. Must be my perception of the Church vs. State doctrine. You absolve crimes in the name of the church. Isn't that a crime in itself?"

The priest remained silent.

"So, how much does absolution cost these days?"

Father Wilkens didn't know Thomas' end-goal.

"We don't have a collection for absolution."

"Who is he?"

"Would you believe me if I told you I don't know?"

Thomas scowled at the priest. "Yes."

Father Wilkens lowered his eyes to the bloody ice pack as he said, "All I ever wanted to be was a priest."

"All I ever wanted to be was a cop," countered Thomas.

"My parents wanted me to be an attorney. They wanted me to help the guilty. So did I."

He leaned toward Thomas. Blood stained his face and clothes.

"I studied law during the day and seminary studies at night. It's not like I had a sex life."

Thomas' body relaxed as the man spoke.

"I became a lawyer. I was miserable. My parents relented and, here I am, helping the guilty."

Thomas explained, "Father Bowden's son raped my daughter. She took a pregnancy test and then committed suicide."

"I'm sorry," the priest said sincerely, eyeing the troubled man.

"Would you take my confession? It's been a while."

Father Wilkens considered the man's request with a furrowed brow and nodded. The priest repeated the words as old as time, "May the Lord be in your heart to help you make a good confession."

"Bless me, Father, for I have sinned. My last confession was one year ago. This is my sin."

"The main thing is that you're seeking reconciliation today."

"I do my job. Crime after crime, there are no mysteries in the end, there are only revelations."

The priest squinted at Thomas.

"Do you feel you've lost your way?"

Thomas looked out the window as he replied, "No, someone showed me the way."

"Go on."

"After Betty Luzer's death, her lawyer sent me a package. It provided a break in the case and she knew that the priest would never report it missing."

"God's listening."

Thomas' voice hardened as he continued, "It was the gun my daughter used to kill herself. A note came with it informing me of that event."

The priest felt the hairs stand up on the back of his neck.

"I'm sorry you had to endure that anguish."

Thomas snorted at the priest. "It was no grief, Father."

"The duty of a policeman can be difficult."

"Being a father is more problematic."

"Why attempt to compare the two?"

"Because, Father, two nights ago I used that gun to kill Father Bowden and Loveta Chilton," Thomas spewed his evil.

The priest reared back in horror. "Oh, my God!"

"I know, right? They say confession is good for the soul. Do you really think that?"

"Let me help you," Father Wilkens offered, grasping the cop with his bloody hand.

Thomas shook the man's hand off, stood, and towered over the priest.

"This isn't about a suicide or homicide. It's about how a priest protected his son after he raped my teenage daughter and then your church covered it up." Thomas tapped his nose twice. "I'm not sorry about that."

"You'll never find peace."

"Maybe, but I'll have my revenge. Pray for him and those protecting him because I'm coming for them, too."

Father Wilkens made the sign of the cross as Thomas exited the study.

"I'll pray for you and your prey." Then the lawyer in him added, "Someone will find the courage to stop you."

"Maybe, but it won't be you."

Thomas exited the church while its bells rang *'Onward Christian Soldier'*.

FBI Special Agent John Treehorn leaned against his vehicle swinging his handcuffs.

"How'd you find me?"

"I'm a federal agent," Treehorn said, meeting the captain's eye, "GPS. Your staff kindly located your vehicle."

"Good detective work. I had a confession to make."

Treehorn's eyes never wavered.

"I get the impression you know more about this case then you're letting on."

"Must be our nature, Agent Treehorn, because I have the same impression from you."

"I guess time will tell," the agent stated matter-of-factly, "Your services are required back at the station."

Thomas entered his precinct, but instead of heading to the conference room he entered the staff work area.

Treehorn leaned casually against the doorframe behind the captain as the man conducted his own song and dance.

Thomas did a two-finger whistle and then spoke loud enough that it garnered everyone's attention.

"I'm duty bound."

The staff eyed each other. Some grinned.

"I need to pass my firearms recertification."

The room erupted. Everyone checked their wallets for cash.

Melanie approached Treehorn and asked, "What's going on?"

"It appears to be a ritual."

Thomas turned and faced Treehorn with a condescending look.

"How's your shooting?"

"Good enough to maintain this gold *FBI* badge."

"I'll tell you what. Let's have a little wager. Just you and I." The man pointed his index finger from man to man.

"I don't gamble," Treehorn stated.

Melanie nodded in agreement.

"Okay, money's off the table. How about something else?" Thomas gave the Fed a cheeky smile.

Treehorn assessed the situation then responded, "I'm listening."

"I win, I get to ask you any question."

"Any question?" Treehorn raised his stitched eyebrow.

"Regarding this investigation."

Treehorn squinted at the captain. "And, when I win?"

Thomas chuckled, doubting he would lose, "Same benefit."

Treehorn glanced at Melanie.

Her eyebrow rose. "Fancy word for *favor*."

Treehorn pushed his suit back and showed his pistol. "You're on!"

The State Police Captain led the group of LEOs and staff into the basement shooting range like a pied piper.

Thomas and Treehorn clipped their paper target on their respective holders and pushed the electronic buttons that sent them down the alley.

The LEOs and staff hurriedly wagered their bets as Melanie placed hers with the 'bookie'.

Then, she stepped to the side to watch the event.

Thomas looked at the female agent and his eyebrow rose as if to ask, "*Who did you wager on?*"

Melanie glanced once at Treehorn and met Thomas' eye. "I want to hear your answer to his question."

Thomas winked at Melanie.

"Six shots, Agent Treehorn."

The two men put on their ear protection, released their pistols' safety, and fired.

The pulley system whined as it returned the two bullet-filled targets to the men.

Half of the crowd cheered as they accepted their winnings.

Thomas' target had five in the inner ring and one touching the next ring.

Half of the crowd grumbled as they paid out their losses.

Treehorn's shots created a six bullet 'cross' in the target's inner circle.

The 'bookie' handed Melanie her winnings as he passed her.

She leaned toward Thomas and whispered, "I've seen that bad boy shoot."

"A warning would have been nice."

"No one bets against my partner, *ever*." Melanie's laughter filled the room.

Treehorn looked at Melanie and nudged his head toward the door. Her exit cue.

"Let me know the question and answer," she said, joining the others upstairs.

"Ask your question," Thomas stated as he refilled his pistol magazine.

Treehorn replaced his clip with a fresh one and returned his gun to its holster.

"I'll ask it when I need an answer."

"Nice shooting. Where'd you learn?"

"I grew up on the Navajo Indian Reservation. Target practice became a hobby."

The examiner handed Thomas his recertification card and patted his shirt pocket where cash stuck.

"Always a pleasure, Captain."

Treehorn eyed the short, gray-haired man.

"You can judge a lot by the faith man puts on another."

He walked away to return to his investigation.

Chapter Eight

I Called My Attorney

Stella Hunter entered the room and ignored Thomas. She walked directly to Treehorn and handed him a set of documents.

"Surrogate's Court sent over a copy of Father Bowden's *Last Will and Testament*."

"Thank You, Ms. Hunter."

"It's Mrs. Hunter, Agent Treehorn."

"I'll remember that."

The agent read the paperwork as the woman left the room, intentionally avoiding her direct supervisor.

Melanie watched Treehorn's focus as she asked, "Anything interesting?"

Her partner handed the first page to Thomas without answering.

Thomas replied to her, "Monies to various charities and one very large life insurance policy to a lady named Eleanor Humphrey."

"She's the retired housekeeper from decades ago," Melanie clarified.

Treehorn finished the legal document stating, "There's no mention of a child."

Glancing at Thomas, Melanie suggested, "A one-night stand?"

Treehorn pursed his lips at his partner.

"The priest may not have *known* he fathered a child," Treehorn said, eyeing Thomas as he drove his point home, "Just like you."

Stella re-entered the room which prevented the captain from commenting.

"Agent Treehorn, Attorney Aaron Robbins and Father Wilkens wish to speak with you. They're waiting in the small conference room."

"Thank you, Mrs. Hunter."

Treehorn pointed to his partner to deal with the documents.

"Take care of them."

"Do you want me to observe?"

"No, this time I want Thomas with me. See what you can find on Eleanor Humphrey."

"Yes, sir," Melanie's flippant attitude returned.

Treehorn and Thomas walked to the interrogation room to greet their visitors.

"What do you think they want?" the agent inquired.

"To catch a killer?" Thomas jested.

"I doubt that," Treehorn stated seriously, as more secrets became exposed in this case.

"Me, too."

The two men stopped outside of the steel door that Troopers Milner and Holmes guarded. Aaron Robbins and Father Wilkens sat together at one end of a table, while Joseph Granger, Gardenia Myers, and Dooley Stiles were grouped together at the other end.

Treehorn observed Joseph Granger. His head was lowered and his hands covered his ears. Gardenia Myers' head remained lowered with her hands over her eyes. Finally, Dooley Stiles' head looked down while his hand covered his mouth.

Trooper Milner remarked, "Look at the three monkeys: Hear no evil, see no evil, speak no evil."

Thomas ordered his officers, "You two stay here in case we need you."

"Ready?" Treehorn asked, glancing at the captain and then entering the room without knocking.

Thomas wondered why the Fed had invited him into the meeting.

Aaron Robbins and Father Wilkens sat at the table with a small box in front of them.

Treehorn observed the priest's swollen face, with a bruised, but not broken, nose. He then glanced at the captain and his right bruised knuckle. He made no comment on the relationship.

Thomas wasn't silent, but instead asked, "Run into a confessional?"

Attorney Robbins snapped, "We're not here to discuss Father Wilkens' mishap!"

The agent eyed the three other guests.

"I'm FBI Special Agent John Treehorn. I'm in charge of this investigation."

Melanie entered the room and positioned herself at the exit.

"My partner, Special Agent Melanie Hopper."

Father Wilkens continued with the newcomers' introductions, "Joseph Granger, Gardenia Myers, and Dooley Stiles."

The three town residents lowered their hands to the table and straightened their spines.

Mr. Robbins pointed to them.

"These individuals each received a package this morning."

Treehorn pulled a latex glove from his pocket, put it on, and lifted the lid of the box. Inside, three stamped and addressed manila envelopes lay opened. Joseph's contained an ear, Gardenia's an eye, and Dooley's a tongue. Each body part appeared to be wrapped in a bloodied diary page.

"Call your lab," Treehorn ordered Thomas.

Melanie stepped forward and examined the box while Thomas made the call.

"Jimmy, the missing body parts of Father Bowden have arrived. Small conference room. Bring a chain of custody form."

"Oh, my God!" Gardenia cried, "They belonged to our priest?"

Treehorn focused on the church's attorney, asking, "Why are you here?"

"I represent the Archdiocese's interest."

The lawyer glanced at the box.

The agent looked at Father Wilkens and repeated the question, "Why are you here?"

"Spiritual guidance," the priest replied, staring at Thomas and not the body parts.

Treehorn whispered something to Thomas and the captain nodded.

Thomas stepped out, whispered something to his troopers, and immediately returned.

Three knocks came on the door.

Treehorn looked at the town folk as he said, "Please follow the officers."

The citizens looked to Attorney Robbins and Father Wilkens for guidance.

"You're going to interrogation rooms for questioning," Treehorn informed them.

Melanie looked at Gardenia and said, "Please come with me."

Attorney Robbins blistered, "They're not to be interviewed without us!"

The three *so-called* pillars of the community stood and followed the police out of the room.

Thomas slammed the door after the last citizen exited.

Treehorn eyed the slick Church attorney, then asked, "Are you representing them?"

"No," Robbins yielded.

Treehorn, a lawyer himself, looked at Father Wilkens.

"Are you licensed to practice law in the State of New York?"

"Yes," the priest replied.

Robbins interrupted, "I object!"

Treehorn stood firm.

"The Church isn't here. I'll allow Father Wilkens in, if they so choose to have counsel."

"This is outrageous! I'm calling your boss," Robbins threatened.

Removing his phone from his pocket Treehorn asked, "Do you want me to dial his number?"

Father Wilkens laid his hand on Robbins' forearm and said reassuringly, "I have this covered."

Jimmy knocked and entered.

Treehorn signed the chain of custody document while Thomas handed the tech the body parts.

Thomas whispered in Jimmy's ear, "Find out what's written on the pages."

"Yes, sir."

Treehorn walked to the door and looked over his shoulder.

"Are you coming, Father?"

Attorney Robbins and William Wilkens' eyes met. The older man motioned toward the door and said, "Do your job."

"Which one?" the priest questioned.

"The one your Church pays you for."

Thomas held the door open for the priest and casually tapped his nose as the man passed.

"You should ice that."

The two men followed far enough behind Treehorn where they couldn't be overheard. As they passed the water fountain the priest pleaded with Thomas, "Let me wash away your sins."

Thomas smirked at Father Wilkens but remained silent.

As they passed the interrogation room of Gardenia Myers and Trooper Holmes, the priest whispered to Thomas, "It's never too late to confess."

"I already did. Do I need to repeat it?"

"I can help you! Tell the police. Admit your guilt."

Thomas stopped the priest by grabbing his sleeve.

"I *am* the police. These three individuals have vital information regarding my daughter's rape investigation. This isn't about me."

"It is now," the priest argued.

Treehorn watched and waited for the two men to finish their tête-à-tête.

Melanie voiced, "I have a feeling they know what's happening and we're the peanut gallery."

"Because you haven't focused on the job," Treehorn replied, raising his stitched eyebrow.

Melanie started to have an active dislike for that catgut in Treehorn's eyebrow.

"I can remove that for you."

The men's arrival prevented the agent's response.

Treehorn opened the door that permitted Thomas and Father Wilkens to enter Interrogation Room #1. The agent touched Melanie's arm and he whispered, "Good cop, bad cop."

Melanie nodded.

Thomas ordered Trooper Milner, "Go keep an eye on Dooley Stiles."

"Yes, sir."

Thomas leaned against the rear wall so he could watch Agent Treehorn operate.

Joseph Granger's black eyes looked at the law enforcement officers with their gold badges and guns. His greasy face shined under the lights and he stayed silent.

Treehorn pressed the button that activated a video recorder.

"I'm FBI Special Agent John Treehorn. Also present in the room is Special Agent Melanie Hopper, St. Philomena Catholic Church's Father William Wilkens, and

New York State Police Captain Thomas Brooks for observation only. Joseph Granger, we're here to ask you about the package you received today, which appears to contain the ear of murder victim Father Howard Bowden. Please state your name for the record."

"Joseph Granger."

"Are you here voluntarily?"

"Yes."

"Father William Wilkens, what position are you representing today?" Treehorn asked for the record.

"I'm here to provide spiritual guidance and act as legal counsel if so requested."

"Mr. Granger, what can you tell us about the Cate Dixon investigation?"

"I thought I was here for the ear I received in the mail?"

"We've uncovered new information that connects Father Bowden's murder with Cate Dixon's case."

Joseph looked at the priest and didn't question the agents' statement.

Treehorn continued, "Can you tell me where you were the night Cate Dixon committed suicide?"

"What does this have to do with me receiving the priest's ear?"

Melanie offered a good cop approach: "Please answer the question."

"I was at my diner."

"Alone?"

"No. Father Bowden was there."

Treehorn carefully worded the next question. "Your diner is located next to the foster home. Did you hear the gunshot?"

"No. Father Bowden and I have already provided sworn statements. We didn't see or hear anything. We were at my diner having a piece of pie."

Melanie gently coaxed, "Why would some sick individual send you the priest's ear?"

"I tell you I didn't see or hear a thing!" Joseph raised his voice.

Treehorn glanced at Thomas and then looked toward Joseph to gauge his reaction.

"Cate Dixon was my daughter." Thomas slowly and distinctly pronounced each word.

Joseph's face paled. He looked at Father Wilkens for guidance but the priest remained silent.

Stella broke the tension in the room as she entered, carrying a manila folder.

"The information you requested, Agent Treehorn."

"Thank you, Mrs. Hunter."

The agent pulled the weapon image from the papers and placed it in front of Joseph for his review.

"Do you recognize this gun?"

The diner owner's eyes shifted away from the photo and then returned to it. "No."

"It's killed three people."

Joseph's focus remained on the gun and he stayed silent.

"Our lab has pulled DNA samples off it."

Joseph's eyebrows furrowed while he appeared lost in thought.

Treehorn observed, "For the record, where were you the night Father Bowden was murdered?"

"I was home, sleeping."

"Were you alone?"

"Yes."

"Why would the priest call you a sinner of the community?"

Joseph clenched his fist and leaned forward.

"I run a diner. I'm an upstanding member of this community. You can ask anyone."

"We have," Thomas added before Treehorn could continue.

Joseph slammed his hand down on the table and yelled, "Is this nightmare ever going to end? I provided a DNA sample. It didn't match."

Melanie interrupted her partner's interrogation, "Did you want to add something about Cate Dixon's investigation?"

Treehorn watched as Joseph clenched his fists and then he asked, "Do you know an E. Humphrey?"

Joseph's eyes didn't move off the gun image as he blurted out, "Never heard of her."

Treehorn's lip curled snarkily.

"Who said it was a woman?"

Father Wilkens raised his hand to the Special Agent. Turning to Granger he said, "That's enough. Joseph, I recommend you ask for an attorney."

Joseph raised his face and smirked at Treehorn, "I want a lawyer."

"You're not under arrest," Melanie stated the fact.

Father Wilkens met Thomas's eye in a silent stand-off.

Treehorn stood.

"You don't have to answer this, but do you have any idea why Father Bowden's killer would send you a piece of the priest?"

Joseph's eyes widened as he comprehended a motive.

"In this FBI Agent's opinion, I think someone sent it as a threat. Trooper Milner will escort you out."

Treehorn stretched out his hand to shake Joseph's hand but the man refused the gesture.

Thomas opened the door so the two men could swiftly exit. As soon as they crossed the threshold, he closed it.

"End of recording," Treehorn said, pressing the device's off button.

Melanie voiced her observation, "Father Wilkens was quiet until Humphreys' name was mentioned."

Thomas countered, "Everyone knows who committed the assault except us."

"What about the murders?" Treehorn asked.

No one offered an answer to his question.

"Let's interview Gardenia Myers next."

Father Wilkens waited for the officers outside of Interrogation Room #2.

Treehorn and Melanie entered while Thomas hung back and whispered to Father Wilkens, "You've been keeping secrets."

"I'm not the only one."

The two men entered the room where Treehorn turned on the recording and introduced everyone for the record.

Father Wilkens sat next to the pale, freckle-faced woman.

"Please state your name for the record."

"Gardenia Myers."

"Are you here voluntarily?"

"Yes."

"What did you see the night of Cate Dixon's suicide?"

"What?" Gardenia looked to Father Wilkens for support.

"Everything will work out. Just answer the officer's questions."

Melanie repeated the question, "What did you see the night of the suicide?"

"I took a walk. I didn't see anything amiss." She sat up straighter in the chair and wiped an invisible speck of dust off her expensive silk sleeve as if brushing away a bad memory, "I gave a report a year ago."

Treehorn informed the snob, "Cate Dixon was Captain Brooks' daughter."

Gardenia's eyes widened in shock as she looked at Thomas and then at Father Wilkens.

The priest offered no response.

Treehorn grilled, "Where were you the night Father Bowden was killed?"

"My husband and I were sleeping."

"Why would someone send you the eye of the priest?" Treehorn grilled.

"I have no idea," Gardenia huffed.

"Did you see something you shouldn't have seen?"

"I have no idea," she lied.

"I think you did see something."

The woman scrunched up her face in anger. "We thought it was bad enough when you Indians claimed our land beneath our church. That's the only reason you're here."

Two Navajo FBI agents silently stared down the woman.

Gardenia looked to the priest for support. None was forthcoming.

Melanie ignored the woman's tirade, "Why would the priest call you a sinner of the community?"

Gardenia answered with a question, "When's this whole mess going to be behind us?"

Treehorn pulled the wooden-handled gun image out of his folder, "Do you recognize this?" Gardenia's mood changed from bitter to excited, "Oh my God! Where did you find it?"

Melanie, with her ATF background, asked, "Do you recognize it?"

"Yes. It was given to my family by the Irish stonemason who built St. Philomena's." She smiled as her finger caressed the photograph, "This gun is part of our town's illustrious history."

"That's the weapon that killed the priest," Treehorn confirmed.

Gardenia reared back in horror.

"What he built, he destroyed," Thomas declared, "You can put *that* in your history book."

The town historian stiffened her spine and raised her nose at everyone.

Father Wilkens offered her an exit. "Is she free to go?" the priest stood up.

"Sit down," Treehorn demanded, pointing Father Wilkens to his seat.

The agent eyed the priest and then Mrs. Myers. The two weren't leaving before he had his questions answered.

"What's your maiden name?"

"Everyone knows it's Humphrey. The family who built this town."

Melanie followed up with, "Are you related to Eleanor Humphrey?"

Gardenia looked to Father Wilkens for help but he appeared to be praying.

"I would like to leave now." She stood.

Treehorn ordered, "Sit down!"

Gardenia again looked to the priest for guidance.

The priest stated. "You can answer it."

She sat and raised her nose. "She's my sister. I haven't spoken to her in years."

Father Wilkens leaned over and whispered something in her ear. Out loud, he stated for the record, "I recommend Gardenia not answer any more of your questions without legal counsel."

Treehorn squinted at her and leaned forward.

"Father Bowden's murderer sent you the priest's eye. He did it for a reason. If there's something you need to tell us, now's a good time."

Gardenia pursed her lips in disgust and stayed silent.

Treehorn waited a few seconds to see whether she would change her mind. She didn't.

"You're free to leave."

Father Wilkens assisted the woman out of the room where Trooper Holmes waited to escort her out of the building.

Treehorn shut off the recorder after the pair departed.

Melanie looked at her partner in surprise and asked, "How did you know she would recognize the gun?"

Treehorn replied, "She published the town's history book which detailed the construction of the church. We knew the gun wasn't manufactured in the States." He then whispered in her ear, "If you were doing your job properly, you would have known that."

"It still doesn't tell us how the gun went from a suicide to a murder."

Thomas started a theory, "What if my daughter told Father Bowden she had been assaulted?"

Treehorn added to the man's idea, "He then confronted the man—who happened to be his son."

Thomas added, "The rapist thought he would be exposed."

Treehorn stated a case fact, "He removed the gun after Cate committed suicide."

Melanie joined in, "The weapon was then used to kill the priest, the only person we assume knew the rapist's identity."

Thomas stated without a doubt, "The rapist is from here."

Treehorn agreed and speculated, "And, so is the killer."

"It doesn't explain why the murderer left the gun," Melanie said, remembering that the two LEOs questioned the reason over coffee at the diner.

Treehorn met Thomas' eye.

"No. It now makes perfect sense. The rapist and killer are two different men."

Thomas' lips pinched slightly with the Special Agent's stare-down.

Treehorn caught the tell.

Melanie processed her partner's theory and the clues that justified it. "The second victim?"

Treehorn filled in a piece of the murder mystery: "Loveta Chilton communicated with the killer." The agent continued to focus on Thomas, "She may have discussed the gun and/or the diary. So, the murderer had to kill her because she could identify him. It's the motive for her death."

"Let's see what Judge Stiles has to offer in this investigation."

Outside of Interrogation Room #3, Treehorn whispered to Melanie, "I want you to start the interview."

Father Wilkens calmly sat at the table while Dooley Stiles bristled and his angry, beady eyes watched as Melanie activated the video.

"Is that necessary?"

Melanie answered, "Yes." She proceeded to list all occupants in the room.

Treehorn pegged the wife beater. The judge's face reddened. He couldn't deal with an educated woman controlling the situation.

Melanie continued, "Can you please state your name for the record?"

Dooley looked at Treehorn and asked with exasperation, "How long are we going to continue with this song and dance?"

Treehorn responded with, "Agent Hopper, can you repeat the question?"

The corner of Melanie's lip lifted as she asked, "Can you state your name for the record?"

"Dooley Stiles," the man spat.

"Are you here voluntarily?"

The big, burly man folded his arms across his chest.

"I'm Special Agent Melanie Hopper and Dooley Stiles refused to answer my question. For the record, he is here voluntarily. It is noted that Mr. Stiles brought with him a United States Postal package, addressed to him, that contains someone's tongue."

Dooley and Melanie conducted a staring contest. Neither backed down.

"Not much of a talker, are you?" she asked, raising her eyebrow.

"People who talk too much usually end up confessing in our line of work."

Melanie prodded, "Do *you* have a confession to make?"

For the first time ever Treehorn appreciated his partner's flippant attitude.

Dooley ignored her.

"Why would someone send you the tongue of the priest?" Melanie inquired on a more serious note.

Dooley looked at Treehorn and answered, "No idea."

Melanie caught the avoidance.

"I think you spoke to someone about a crime."

Dooley offered no response or eye contact.

She refused to relent, asking, "Where were you the night Cate Dixon committed suicide?"

Dooley smiled at a memory as he glanced at Thomas.

The State Police knew the man's history. It was no secret. Thomas provided the man's alibi to the room's occupants, "I believe we've already established that this upstanding pillar of the community was at home beating his wife."

Dooley pounded his fists on the table.

"Good luck proving that."

Father Wilkens lowered his head as if praying for the abuser's soul.

Changing the route of questioning, Treehorn asked,

"Do you know Eleanor Humphrey?"

Dooley's fists and face relaxed.

"It's been a long time since I heard her name spoken."

Melanie pressed, "Was she the first woman who thought you were pathetic?"

Dooley's cruel eyes focused on Melanie as he replied sincerely, "Eleanor understood me."

Melanie felt her neck hairs rise.

"And why was that?"

"She made me realize I wasn't the cause of my problems."

"Really?" Melanie couldn't contain her sarcasm.

Treehorn placed a finger on Melanie's back out of everyone's eyesight except Thomas'. A professional sign that silently conveyed he now controlled the interrogation.

"Do you know who raped Cate Dixon?"

"No," came Dooley's brusque reply.

Thomas informed, "She was my daughter."

The judge's face appeared indifferent as he glanced at Father Wilkens.

"Do you know why anyone would murder the priest and his housekeeper?"

"No clue."

"Did anyone share anything in your capacity as a judge about these crimes that would assist us in our investigation?"

"No one."

Treehorn repeated his partner's earlier question, "Why did Father Bowden's killer mail you the priest's tongue?"

"I haven't a clue," Dooley nonchalantly replied.

"I would have to agree."

Melanie smiled at Treehorn's uncharacteristically witty response.

"I'm a small-town judge. So, what if I'm known for giving petty criminals a pass?" Dooley sneered, forgetting his environment during his ego boost.

A look of disgust crossed Father Wilkens' face. The lawyer in him found his conscience.

Treehorn stared at the elected official. His face showed no emotion.

"No, you're a dirty judge in a small town. It appears the only criminals who receive a deal are the domestic abusers."

Dooley leaned toward Melanie as he said, "We have to stick together."

She glanced down at the red blinking light on the video recorder, tilted her head at the abuser, and grinned.

Dooley wasn't too bright as he literally foretold his future, "I'm still the judge in this town and I'm done here."

Melanie chuckled, "Yes, you are."

Treehorn turned off the recorder.

"When I return to Washington, I will recommend a Federal investigation to examine every case in which you rendered a verdict."

"Good luck with that."

Thomas leaned forward as he clarified, "I was promised a favor by the Governor's office and I plan on collecting. You're going down."

Dooley grunted like a pig.

Melanie couldn't contain her laughter.

The judge bared his teeth at her, asking snarkily, "What are you laughing at?"

"These men are going to take a pig like you and turn you into bacon."

Dooley stood and spat at Father Wilkens.

"Thanks for *nothing*!"

Melanie's flippant attitude reappeared, "Come on, Stooley, I'll show your bacon to the front door."

"It's Judge Stiles," Dooley corrected her as he stormed out.

Treehorn held up his hand to Melanie.

"Trooper Milner, would you please escort Judge Stiles out of the building?"

Melanie raised her eyebrow.

Treehorn walked away without commenting and she followed him.

Father Wilkens and Captain Brooks, adversaries, stared at each other.

The priest wanted to know, "When did you steal the diary?"

"Who said I stole it?"

"How did you come to be in possession of it?"

"Would you believe me if I told you someone literally handed it to me?"

"Is there no end to your crimes?" Father Wilkens grabbed his arm and pleaded, "Please stop!"

Thomas shook the man's hand off, instead asking, "Tell me who Bowden's son is and this will end today. I know you can identify him."

"His name's not in the diary?" The father saved the son.

"No, just referenced."

"I'm going to find him and I don't care how many of your sinners I need to bring to their knees to accomplish it."

The priest looked at the time.

"I have a mass to perform."

"You need to tell them that I'm coming for him."

The captain watched Father Wilkens as he walked away. His religious frock swirled around him but Thomas knew it wouldn't protect him.

The priest stopped, looked back at Cate's father, and made the sign of the cross on his chest.

Thomas walked to the fountain where he stopped to rinse his face with cold water. A *Lady Justice* mural covered the wall. Fitting, because she stared unseen, outward to all. He examined the details of the woman's blindfold, a balance in one hand, and the sword in the other.

Melanie softly whispered, "Do you believe justice is blind?"

"The day I graduated from the New York State Police Academy and received this uniform was my greatest achievement. I choose to wear this because its threads are woven of equal parts white and black to symbolize the impartiality of justice."

Thomas looked at Melanie's black suit worn over a crisp white shirt and raised his eyebrow.

"Treehorn says everything is black and white." The agent lifted her pant leg. "He's told me to wear grey socks to show there's a fine line between the two. No one sees it. You haven't answered my question."

"I didn't believe it until a year ago, when I went from upholding the law to being on the other side, a victim of circumstance."

"Treehorn won't stop until the perpetrators are caught. You understand that, right?"

"What I want is the man who assaulted my daughter to be hung from a rope."

Melanie watched as Thomas walked away. One day, she'd tell him how she understood.

Treehorn, Melanie, and Thomas acknowledged Jimmy's arrival as he entered the conference room carrying evidence bags with their supporting documentation.

"What do we have?" Treehorn asked.

"The copies of the diary pages that wrapped the body parts," the lab tech said, handing them to the man in charge, "The handwriting matched Father Bowden's."

Treehorn examined each and then handed them to Melanie.

Jimmy detailed his results, "Two pages were wrapped around the eye, one each for the ear and tongue. The murderer's a sick killer, but the locals described on these pages are worse."

"People are devious, Jimmy, when they have an agenda that needs to be met," Thomas stated.

"After reading these papers, all I have to say is *there's a psychiatric unit missing some of their patients.*"

Treehorn didn't comment on the mental illness of the described individuals or their behaviors.

Jimmy looked at the lead agent and asked, "Can I return to my cave, Agent Treehorn?"

"Do we have any results on the knife that stabbed the priest?"

Jimmy shook his head.

"I'll check on it for you and message you an update."

"Thanks."

Treehorn read the first page labeled *'Ear'*: *"I was given a gun a long time ago. I gave it to the girl. I knew he wasn't going to stop, so I had to help her. God help me."*

Melanie glanced at it and handed it to Thomas.

"Can we assume Father Bowden gave your daughter the gun?"

"Maybe."

Treehorn's face tightened with anger as he flipped to the next evidence bag *'Eye'*: *She watched from the window and stated his hands were all over her. I told him I could watch or call the police. I could not believe such sin existed in my flock."*

Melanie's face pinched with disgust as she read the page. *"He raped her. I can still hear her screams. He threatened to expose me."* Father Bowden wrote, *"I asked her to go to the police, but she refused."* "She's sick and she's a witness." Melanie knew realistically the LEOs now faced two hard facts.

Thomas said the first, "They knew about the crimes and did nothing."

Treehorn voiced the second, the dashing of unrealistic hopes of men, "The Separation of Church and State. These

148

documents will never see the light of a courtroom." He read the last page labeled *'Tongue':* *"I asked him how someone could get away with a crime and he told me what I had to do. I'm ashamed of my part in this deceit."*

Melanie added, "We can't match a single soul to these pages."

Treehorn being the realist said, "We have the one thing that will convict him: his DNA."

"You're right. DNA doesn't lie.

Chapter Nine

Eleanor Humphrey

Melanie and Troopers Milner and Holmes entered the conference room with documents and coffee.

"We have background information," Trooper Milner said, pinning a driver's license to the bulletin board.

'Eleanor Humphrey', age 65. A grey-haired, neatly dressed woman. "Image taken a year ago."

Holmes followed, "Retired ten years. Never married. One sister: Gardenia Myers. Her employment records prior to the church were incomplete. She worked twenty-five years for the church before her retirement."

Treehorn asked, "Is she still at this address?"

"Yes, it's a convent in Burlington, Vermont."

Trooper Holmes added, "She worked at a boarding school in Pennsylvania for a year."

Thomas' face showed puzzlement as he asked, "When was that?"

"Her third year at the rectory," Holmes provided the date.

Treehorn's lip curled.

"Do you know what the church sometimes called their boarding schools?"

Thomas replied, "Homes for unwed mothers."

Melanie offered, "I'll pull the records from Pennsylvania."

Treehorn questioned the outcome, "Do you think this woman gave birth to the priest's son?"

"One way to find out," Melanie replied, typing on her laptop.

"See who's listed on the birth certificate," Treehorn ordered.

"He won't be listed," Thomas gave his opinion, "The church wouldn't have allowed it."

"The child's name will be listed. Then we can determine whether his DNA matches."

"Then, he'll be arrested for his crimes."

"Crimes? My opinion hasn't changed. Two men committed these crimes."

Thomas disagreed, silently raising his eyebrow. The special agent refused to back down while his eyes showed no emotion.

"Call it FBI intuition."

"Good work today, Agent Treehorn," Thomas said, glancing at his timepiece, "I have an appointment. See you tomorrow." The captain took the time to whisper something to Melanie before he departed.

Treehorn watched as his partner smiled. He didn't.

Neither did Dr. Mario Mancini as he stared at Thomas from his seat behind his desk.

"Why the quick departure?"

"I had to see a priest about a confession. It put my job into…perspective."

Dr. Mancini eyed the captain over his bifocals as he asked, "Did it help?"

Thomas snorted, "Everyone thinks I'm grieving for my daughter."

"Not everyone."

Thomas smirked at the psychiatrist.

"I'm a cop. You understand crime because you're a forensic psychiatrist. Tell me again, why do you see live and dead patients?"

"I like working with both. It gives me…perspective."

Thomas sighed.

Dr. Mancini empathized, "I'm trying to understand how I can treat you."

"Do I need help? Because from where I'm sitting, I don't see it that way."

"Would you have walked in that door if it wasn't job-ordered?"

"No."

"What answer do you search for?"

"Sadly, it's one that will never be answered. Why?"

"I'm sure this isn't the first crime you've asked that and it won't be the last."

Thomas knew those truths.

"The priest had a son and DNA proved that man raped my daughter."

"This is a break in the case you've needed for months."

"The priest never told me what he knew."

"Did he keep silent because he was a man of the cloth?"

"No, I believe he kept silent because he truly was evil."

"Does it change anything?"

"No, but it's ironic. His death's helping to solve a rape, but not his homicide."

"There's no statute of limitations on murder."

"The killer knows this, too."

Thomas glanced out the window and noticed the rain had stopped. He wondered whether it was an omen, because he felt like he needed one.

Thomas and Melanie entered the station carrying coffee and donuts. The station was unusually abuzz with activity for a Thursday morning.

Treehorn looked at the pair and greeted them, "Good morning."

Melanie winked. "It is."

Treehorn squinted and explained, "We received the birth record information."

"The bad news?" Thomas asked.

"Sealed," the agent replied.

Melanie joined, "Let's assume Miss Humphrey gave up the child since we haven't found any records of her raising an infant."

Treehorn eyed the pair.

"What do you suggest, Agent Hopper?"

"Let's go interview her," Melanie proposed.

"What makes you think she'd discuss her history with you?" Treehorn countered.

"We have nothing to lose by confronting her."

Thomas suggested, "You could ask her why Father Bowden left her a large sum of money."

"And then ask her who knocked her up?"

Melanie's humor disappeared when she saw Treehorn's angry face.

The senior agent repeated his mantra, *"Do your job."*

Thomas refereed, "I'm interested in learning the identity of the father. We're assuming it's the priest."

"You could be wrong."

"Possibly. We'll inform her the priest had a son who's a rapist."

"See if she's inclined at that point to provide us with an answer," Treehorn requested.

"We'll either learn the identity of Cate's assailant or we'll continue the search for him."

Treehorn looked at the pair and ordered, "Thomas, you and Agent Hopper interview her. Ask Ms. Humphrey whether Father Bowden had any enemies who would have wanted him dead. I'll work on the sealed record while you're gone."

"I'll call you when we're done," Melanie said.

She gave Treehorn a French salute. His pursed lips indicated he caught her action.

After the two departed, Treehorn telephoned the Archdiocese's attorney.

"Attorney Aaron Robbins speaking."

"Special Agent John Treehorn."

"Why the call?"

"I'm meeting Judge Dick Persky in two hours. Do you wish to attend the meeting?"

"What's the purpose?"

"I'm requesting the unsealing of Father Bowden's adoption records. You're welcome to come and challenge the case."

"I'll give it some thought," the attorney stated before the call terminated.

Treehorn's lip curled. The lawyer just verified what the FBI agent suspected. The Church knew the priest had fathered a son.

Two hours later, FBI Special Agent John Treehorn and Attorney Aaron Robbins sat in front of Judge Persky.

The sixty-year-old man sat behind a hand-crafted oak desk, not in a black robe but a buttoned-up oxford shirt with a child's hand-painted tie.

Treehorn glanced at the tie and then met the judge's stare.

"Grandson."

The judge examined the legal petition, asking, "Please explain the request to unseal a legal adoption in Pennsylvania."

"I'm lead FBI agent on Father Bowden's murder investigation. One year ago, a fourteen-year-old teenager in foster care named Cate Dixon committed suicide. DNA testing this week proved that the priest, Howard Bowden, fathered a child who raped and impregnated the girl."

The judge eyed the Church attorney who sat silently.

"How do you know this birth certificate is his?"

"We don't. We do know that the woman on record, Eleanor Humphrey, lived with Father Bowden at the time. I believe she gave birth at a Catholic boarding school in Pennsylvania. Upon Father Bowden's death, Miss Humphrey was named primary beneficiary. He left a note regarding the money that stated, '*For you and ours.*'"

"This is a fishing expedition, Agent Treehorn?"

"Yes, it is."

"So, this is pure speculation that Father Bowden fathered the child on this birth record?"

"True," the agent provided the straightforward answer.

The judge once again looked at the silent Church attorney and then back to the Special Agent.

"How will you obtain this information if I don't sign this petition?"

"I'll personally knock on every household in the area, inform them that not only did Father Bowden have a son who's a rapist, but that the priest kept a diary of confessions, too."

The judge's eyes rounded as he glared at the attorney. "A diary?"

Attorney Robbins cleared his throat. Finally deciding to participate he offered, "I can't tell you whether the priest fathered a child. That would be against attorney/client privilege. The Church can't tell me because that would go against Canon Law."

The judge glanced at the reserved Special Agent who just outsmarted a slick lawyer.

Attorney Robbins continued, "Nice maneuver and thanks for the invite, Agent Treehorn." He then looked at the judge, adding, "The Feds have kept the contents of the diary under wraps and the Church is grateful. Unofficially, the church would support the release of this document rather than having this agent informing citizens about Father Bowden's misdeeds."

"And officially?"

"I'm Agent Treehorn's invited guest." Spoken with a forked tongue.

Treehorn eyed the seminary ring on the judge's right hand.

"We want his identification to hunt down a rapist. That's the bottom line."

Judge Persky signed the subpoena. He didn't ink his signature because of the Special Agent's lack of evidence supporting the warrant, but because the Church's lawyer didn't challenge it. The Catholic in him would never confess that. The judge handed the agent the legal document. "Are we done?"

"I have an FBI matter to discuss." Treehorn informed the judge. He opened the door to allow Attorney Robbins to exit the chambers.

"I'll say it again: Nice maneuver. Why do I feel dirty?"

Treehorn stepped into the man's personal space as he said, "Probably, because you are. Did you forget I'm an attorney who's licensed to practice law in the State of New York?"

Robbins took a step back. "Would you really have knocked on every residence?"

"To hunt down a rapist? You have to ask?" Agent Treehorn raised his eyebrow and watched as the Church's lawyer exited the room.

Treehorn returned to Judge Persky and handed him a warrant request. The agent sat while the judge read every detail of the request and its supporting documentation.

The judge didn't ask a single question upon finishing it, but took a long and hard stare at the Native American FBI agent. A stranger in their midst. He scrawled his signature across the bottom of the legal document without commenting and returned the paper to the Fed.

"Thank you, your Honor." Special Agent folded the document and then placed it in his front pants pocket next to his gold badge.

Judge Persky pointed to the door. "Good luck with your arrest."

Thomas and Melanie discussed their cases during the two-hour drive to the Sisters of St. Mary Convent. A bitter wind blew off Lake Champlain as the two LEOs approached the large granite convent.

As the agent rang the front bell, a tiny iron flap at eye level opened on the door.

A nun of approximately thirty years of age eyed the officers.

"Yes?"

Presenting her federal identification, the agent said, "I'm FBI Special Agent Melanie Hopper and this is New York State Police Captain Thomas Brooks. We're here to speak with Eleanor Humphrey."

The nun's eyes went to Thomas.

"He'll have to stay outside. Only women are allowed in."

"Do you know why Treehorn wanted me out of his hair?"

Melanie shook her head and appeared apologetic.

"I'll pick up lunch while you're interviewing her."

"Thanks, I'll try to be finished by the time you return."

"No hurry."

Melanie watched him walk away and wondered what Treehorn's agenda had become.

The nun opened the door and Melanie entered an opulent hallway. The sister who was dressed in full black garb, trimmed in white, immediately relocked the entrance door.

Melanie listened to the nun as she spoke into an in-house telephone.

"You have a visitor." The woman paused, "The FBI," and then she hung up the handset.

"This place is beautiful," Melanie whispered with reverence.

The woman stated, "We're a silent order."

The agent quietly followed the young sister as they traveled several hallways to reach the private apartments. They passed several nuns all dressed in black and white habits. Everyone except Melanie walked with their eyes lowered.

The nun pointed to an old wooden bench.

"When you're finished, wait here, and I'll escort you out."

The sister silently pointed to Apartment #2 and then walked away.

Melanie knocked on the door with her identification in her hand.

A woman who matched the driver's license on record opened the door. Her pastel blouse matched her grey skirt and hair perfectly. There was no welcoming smile.

"Eleanor Humphrey?"

The woman nodded and replied, "Yes."

"FBI Special Agent Melanie Hopper. May I come in?"

Eleanor's fingers whitened on the door, but she allowed the agent entrance into her living room before gently closing it.

Melanie secured the space with her engrained law enforcement background.

"I was having tea, would you like some?"

"Yes please."

Melanie's eyes traveled around the apartment, taking in the woman's history. Two faded lines on the wall showed the outline of a pair of picture frames.

Observing the woman's focus Eleanor explained, "They fell and their glass broke. It takes time to repair some things."

Melanie waited until the woman was seated on the sofa then explained, "I'm investigating a rape that occurred in Altona over a year ago."

The teacup that Eleanor held shook slightly as she handed it to Melanie.

"Sad business. I thought you were here to investigate Father Bowden's murder?"

"I am. Do you know of anyone who wanted the priest dead?"

"No, but who would kill a priest?"

"We're speculating that Father Bowden knew the killer and he was murdered to keep their secrets."

"Do you have any suspects?"

"I'm not at liberty to discuss specifics of the investigation."

"I understand."

"Why did Father Bowden leave you a large sum of money in his will?"

"We were friends," the woman said, picking invisible lint off her clothing.

"We know you spent time at a home for unwed mothers."

"They were in need of help, so I volunteered."

Eleanor's fingers clenched her skirt.

"The DNA lab has determined that Father Bowden fathered a son."

"Sad. Nothing's sacred anymore."

"Let's focus on the rape victim. You see Father Bowden's son left his victim pregnant."

Eleanor closed her eyes.

"A baby?" The woman's face changed from pale to a sickly shade of grey.

"Yes. Who is he?"

"My pills!" Eleanor grabbed for her purse.

"Do you need a glass of water?"

She nodded.

"Please," she said, pointing Melanie to the bathroom as she opened her pill container.

Melanie rushed to fill a cup with cold water. Glancing down, she noticed a bundle of hair in the garbage can.

Eleanor accepted the water from the agent and quickly swallowed her medicine.

Melanie watched as the color returned to the woman's face.

"Do you need me to call your doctor?"

The woman shook her head.

"If you don't assist us, we'll track him down using his birth record."

"Those records are sealed."

"We'll obtain a court order."

Eleanor looked out the window and watched poetically as the storm clouds lined the sky. "You won't need to unseal them."

The two women faced off.

"I gave her up for adoption."

"A girl?"

"Yes."

"Was Howard Bowden the father?"

Eleanor walked to her front door and opened it.

"What do you think?" Her eyes shimmered with anger, "I'd like you to leave now!"

Melanie glanced one last time at the wall where the pictures had hung. She handed Eleanor her contact information as she exited.

"Please call me if you change your mind and want to catch Father Bowden's killer. We're wondering if the priest's son murdered him to protect his identity."

"Get out!"

Eleanor slammed the door and then viciously ripped the business card to pieces.

Melanie sat patiently on the bench until the silent nun arrived to escort her from the building.

Thomas watched the female agent return to his vehicle while deep in thought.

"Did Ms. Humphrey provide any answers?"

"She gave birth to a girl."

Thomas frowned. "Not a boy?"

"I'm sorry. We won't identify the man who assaulted your daughter today."

"Agent Treehorn isn't going to be happy."

"The man's never happy, so today won't be any different."

Melanie sent a text to the Burlington, Vermont FBI field office requesting a garbage pickup at the Sisters of St. Mary Convent.

"I think she's hiding something." The agent gave her opinion to Thomas.

Melanie telephoned Treehorn.

"Treehorn."

"Eleanor Humphrey admitted she gave birth to a girl."

"Then, we'll have to find the rapist another way."

Chapter Ten

David Nathan Allen

Treehorn examined the bulletin board after he faxed the judge's order to Pennsylvania. Two murders and an assault. A gun and DNA connected the cases. A puzzle. The Church had the answers and the agent sensed the community did, too. Why protect a perpetrator? Why didn't the citizens come forth when the assault occurred? Too many questions and not enough answers.

The telephone rang.

"Treehorn."

"Jimmy. We received the DNA results from the gun. One belonged to Cate Dixon and the other a male. I compared his DNA to Cate's fetus and it's a match for the father."

"Who is it?"

"I'm sending the results to your computer."

"Thanks, Jimmy."

As Treehorn waited for the download he told everyone present, "The lab matched the male DNA on the gun to Cate's baby."

"That'll identify the rapist," Trooper Milner stated, "If he's in the system."

"He'll be the next felon arrested in the State of New York," Trooper Holmes added.

The three LEOs watched as a mug shot of a bearded, menacing man covered the screen.

Treehorn commented, "*David Nathan Allen*, son of a priest."

"Looks like a real keeper." Trooper Milner's sarcasm was duly noted.

David Allen, age thirty-five. A police mug shot showed a pale, shaggy-bearded biker-type dressed in a black leather jacket. His green eyes, one blackened, appeared menacing as he stared angrily at the photographer. The image held a permanent watermark that read, "*STATE of PENNSYLVANIA - Allegheny County Jail.*"

Treehorn read his police record, "Mr. Allen hasn't been a model citizen. He pleaded guilty to a misdemeanor child endangerment charge. Served nine months." The agent scrolled down the file. "He had no priors and his genetic material wasn't in the database at the time of the crimes."

"*DNA MATCH*" appeared on the screen.

"Find him!" the agent ordered.

"Yes, sir."

Treehorn sent Melanie a text with the case update.

Melanie repeated the information to Thomas, "Jimmy's identified Father Bowden's son, who was Cate's rapist."

"The birth record?"

"No, DNA from the gun."

Thomas reached for his daughter's cross in his pocket, pulled it out, and kissed it.

Melanie activated the SUV's emergency lights.

"Floor it. I know Treehorn. He'll have the man's location by the time we arrive."

Treehorn telephoned his communications department in Washington DC and they issued an all-points bulletin for the suspect. His staff accessed the man's financial records, too. When Thomas and Melanie entered the precinct, her co-worker had secured the needed information.

"He's renting a house south of Ray Brook, approximately two hours from here. Get changed into tactical gear."

"Our Troop B headquarters is located there. You don't need to pull your Feds," Thomas offered, "I can have as many officers as you need to apprehend him."

Treehorn silently questioned the timeframe as he handed the captain the perpetrator's address and said, "Do it!"

Thomas coordinated their arrival with other State Police. They met four miles from the single-story residence, at a local Methodist church parking lot.

Reconfirming that his pocket held the arrest warrant, Treehorn said to Thomas, "Stay behind me. I don't want any procedural conflict as we apprehend him."

"I understand, Agent Treehorn," Thomas's voice clipped, "My men know the rules, also. You're in charge."

Treehorn spoke into his microphone as he checked his weapon, "Consider him armed and dangerous."

The special agent drove to the front of the house while the others formed a protective barricade around the area. All of the officers wore their black fatigues with 'STATE POLICE' labeled on their vests while Treehorn's and Melanie's held the dark gold, 'FBI'.

Treehorn and Melanie pulled out their pistols and said in unison, "Let's do this!"

The State Police approached the front door with a ramming tool and waited for the Special Agent.

Treehorn pounded on the front entrance.

"FBI. We have an arrest warrant. Open the door!"

Silence. He motioned for the State Police to break it down.

When the iron ram struck the door for the first time, the wooden frame holding it splintered into different-sized pieces.

Treehorn and the officers rushed into the house with their weapons drawn.

The FBI and State Police stepped over trash and beer cans as they swept the residence in an organized search pattern for the suspect.

"He's not here, sir."

The officers holstered their weapons and continued to search for clues as a rust-colored tabby cat meowed.

"He can't be all bad if he owns a cat," Melanie said matter-of-factly.

Thomas opened his mouth to make an offhand comment but stopped when he found Treehorn staring directly at him.

Melanie watched her partner's glare transfer from Thomas to her. As Treehorn walked past her, she heard him snort.

"What is your problem?" she angrily whispered.

Treehorn ignored her.

"David Allen's first felony arrest occurred near here at a bar called…"

"…Hank's Hideaway," Thomas interrupted, grabbing one of the used matchbooks that littered the coffee table, "My officers have made several arrests there over the years. The establishment is a few miles further down the road."

"Leave a couple unmarked cars here in case he returns," Treehorn ordered as he walked out.

Any police department rookie would know that the neon sign outlining a naked woman that illuminated *Hank's Hideaway* wasn't for the casual, law-abiding citizen who wanted to take in a cold one. A few motorcycles and late-model cars dotted the parking lot.

Thomas looked at the establishment and said somberly, "I wish to go in alone."

Treehorn's eyes met Melanie's in the passenger seat.

This time, it was her eyebrow that raised.

"Nothing wrong with having a beer, right?" Thomas kidded.

Treehorn spoke into his microphone, "Agent Treehorn here. Secure the perimeter. *Mr.* Brooks is going into the building alone."

"Wait here," Thomas ordered Treehorn, who didn't react to the request.

Melanie watched as the captain walked into the bar and then looked at Treehorn with his normal stoic expression, "Do you want him dead?"

Treehorn curled his lip and asked his FBI partner with a cryptic message, "Who doesn't want the rapist and murderer apprehended?"

As they secured the rear entrance, Troopers Holmes and Milner watched their captain exit the FBI Chevy Tahoe and enter the establishment without police backup.

Trooper Milner covered his microphone to ask, "Which one do you think is crazier?"

Trooper Holmes covered her mouthpiece to answer, "I think it's become a competition."

Thomas entered the bar wearing a black jacket that covered his *STATE POLICE*-labeled bulletproof vest. He stood in the middle of the room with his thumbs hooked on his belt.

The men and women in the bar recognized the cop's arrival by his stance and the authority that cloaked him. Their conversations abruptly ceased.

175

Thomas took his time to scope out the joint and its occupants.

Their expressions ranged from smirks to anger to anticipation of violence.

Some considerate soul pulled the jukebox electrical cord from the wall.

Thomas spoke to the group, "I'm looking for a man who raped a fourteen-year-old girl."

Some faces showed disgust at the disclosure. No one came forward and no one asked for the man's identity.

The bartender pulled a bat from beneath the bar and slammed it down on the counter. The two men eyed each other.

"Hello, Hank."

The fifty-year-old grizzly, sharp-eyed bartender didn't offer a greeting but instead tightened his grip on the Louisville slugger.

"The place is surrounded. You can cooperate or not."

The patrons looked out the windows and spotted the police vehicles.

Thomas approached Hank and reached into his front pocket.

The sound of a revolver being cocked drew everyone's attention to the action and then to Ross, a potbellied balding biker dude, who held a handgun pointed to the captain's head.

Thomas and Hank's eyes met. Neither flinched.

A chill came across the bar as another joined the fray.

Ross felt the pistol's barrel as it pressed against his skull.

"Shoot him and you'll be dead before he hits the floor," Treehorn's cold words issued the reality.

The biker immediately lowered his weapon because he heard the truth in the man's voice.

Hank shoved the bat into Ross' stomach.

"You'll never learn like these guys."

Thomas grabbed the bat while Treehorn removed the weapon from Ross' grip.

"On your knees and place your hands behind your back."

The pistol remained pressed against Ross' head until he kneeled and readied his wrist for Treehorn's handcuffs. Then the agent's hand pressed on the man's shoulder, "Stay down," Treehorn said, holstering his weapon.

Thomas glared at Treehorn.

"I told you to wait in the vehicle."

"You didn't clarify for how long."

The cheeky bartender chuckled at the FBI-vested man as he asked, "Buddies?"

When he received only cold stares, he changed his tactic, asking, "Who are you looking for?"

Thomas pulled out David Allen's photo and placed it on the counter.

Hank examined it and nodded.

"Come with me."

Treehorn motioned for Melanie to stay with the handcuffed prisoner.

"Read him his rights."

The three men tread softly down the darkened hallway, lit only by a worn-out exit sign that cast an eerie red glow on the men's faces as they passed beneath it.

"How are you, Hank?" Thomas asked softly.

"Same ol', same ol'. You?"

"I returned to work this week."

"That's why I haven't seen you at your camp."

Treehorn caught the drift. These two men knew each other.

The three came upon a huge muscular man who guarded the room's entrance.

"Step aside," Hank ordered.

The big guy stared at the LEOs and didn't budge.

"My boss pays me to stand here."

He opened his jacket and showed a knife. Before the man's jacket fell back into place Treehorn pulled his pistol from its holster and placed it against the man's head.

"I know its cliché, but never bring a knife to a gun fight. Now, move away from the door."

The man looked into Treehorn's eyes and what he saw made him step aside.

Thomas pulled out his pistol and aimed it at the guard.

"I got this one. Go get him."

Treehorn stopped Hank from reaching for the knob.

"I have this."

The sound of the door opening drew the attention of the five male poker players.

"FBI Special Agent John Treehorn. Raise your hands and don't make any sudden moves."

Hank voiced his opinion behind the agent, "We don't want any trouble."

Troopers Holmes and Milner entered from the emergency exit behind the bar owner.

Hank pointed to the man with his back to Treehorn.

"David Nathan Allen?" the Fed tapped his barrel on the man's shoulder.

"Yes."

"You're under arrest. Do you have any weapons on you?"

"No."

"Stand and place your hands behind your back."

The man complied and Trooper Milner handed Treehorn a pair of handcuffs.

"It's never wise to sit with your back to the door," the Fed stated as the cuffs locked.

"I haven't broken any laws unless you consider a private game of poker a crime."

"We'll see."

Treehorn looked at the four other men in the room and the large amounts of money on the table.

"Holmes, grab their identifications."

"Do you want us to arrest them?"

The agent memorized each of their faces including the man in the tailored suit.

"No, only if they have outstanding warrants. Today's their lucky day."

The rich guy nodded respectfully to Treehorn.

"We have what we came for," The Fed said, turning David Allen around to face Thomas, "Do you want the other man charged? Your call."

"No."

Thomas shook his head as he stared at the man arrested for his daughter's assault.

"He's enough for now."

The perpetrator eyed Thomas, all dressed in black, and spat, "I want a lawyer!"

"We can arrange that."

Treehorn read the man his Miranda rights as he walked him to his SUV.

Thomas and Hank stayed in the darkened hallway as the others moved away.

Hank asked, "We're cool here?"

"We're fine," Thomas affirmed, shaking Hank's hand.

"I hope he's your man."

"I do, too."

Thomas entered the bar area and removed the handcuffs from Ross.

"Today's your lucky day, too. If you ever point a gun at me again, I'll put you in your grave."

Then, he gave the man a mighty shove.

The State Police waited for their orders.

"We're done here. Milner, I'll ride with you."

The team followed their Captain's orders without commenting.

Treehorn placed David in the rear seat and handcuffed his hands to the front security bar. "Do you have your lawyer's number?"

"It's on my phone."

Melanie removed David's device from the evidence bag and placed it in his hand.

"You get one phone call. You'll be at the New York State Police substation in Altona in two hours."

Treehorn appeared deep in thought as he watched the man from his position outside the SUV.

"What are you thinking?" Melanie questioned, noticing her partner's serious expression.

"That a murderer is still running free."

"You can't win them all, Treehorn."

The senior agent glared at Melanie and snapped, "Do your job and we may catch a killer!"

Her flinch didn't go unnoticed by Treehorn.

"I'm leaving here this weekend whether he's been caught or not," she snapped back.

"You'll be flying to Detroit this weekend," Treehorn stated.

"Why?"

Flying was the one thing Melanie hated about her job.

"FBI business. Keep it to yourself."

David waved his phone to get the Fed's attention.

Treehorn opened the rear door to curtail any questions.

"My lawyer's away. Legal aid is sending his replacement."

Treehorn returned the man's phone to the evidence bag and observed one thing. The perp didn't look at all concerned about his arrest.

The FBI agents and their prisoner stayed silent during the return trip to the station. Each lost in their own thoughts regarding this investigation.

Treehorn and Thomas stared at David Nathan Allen through the one-way glass of the interrogation room.

The detainee sat relaxed while supervised by Trooper Milner.

"DNA says we got our man," Thomas stated, "Did he confess?"

"No, he just requested a lawyer."

Treehorn once again focused on the relaxed prisoner as he noted, "He doesn't look too upset to be facing state prison."

Thomas took a long look at the prisoner confirming, "No, he doesn't."

Treehorn observed Thomas' tightened posture.

Stella broke the men's concentration as she entered the secured room.

Treehorn caught the smirk on her face directed at Thomas as she said, "His lawyer's here."

"Send him in," the captain ordered as his gaze returned to the detainee.

Father Wilkens entered the room carrying a briefcase. His dark suit and white tie similarly matched his previous priest attire. The swelling on his face had reduced to a slight puffiness, while the previously blackened bruises had changed their hue.

"I'd like to see my client."

Treehorn and Thomas' eyes met and then turned to the priest-cum-lawyer.

The captain spoke before the agent, "Quit your day job?"

"I'm volunteering my skills at the local legal aid agency."

Treehorn asked next, "Isn't this a conflict between the separation of Church and State?"

Father Wilkens countered the agent, "I don't see how."

The lawyer in Treehorn wasn't going to have this case dismissed on a technicality.

"I will allow you to see him if you inform him that you're St. Philomena's assigned priest."

Father Wilkens' lips rose into a smile, but the emotion didn't reach his eyes.

"Agreed."

Treehorn stepped inside the interrogation room to update the assailant and trooper.

Thomas pointed to a hallway table outside the door where a wooden container sat.

"You can place your briefcase in the box. Please empty your pockets and place the device inside the briefcase. Only a pad and pen are allowed with your client."

Trooper Holmes stood a few feet away waiting for her orders.

Thomas leaned into Father Wilkens' space and whispered, "You're a man of many talents."

The priest spat back, "I don't want you to frame an innocent man!"

Trooper Milner exited the room and stood with Trooper Holmes in case their services were required.

Treehorn turned on the video recorder inside the interrogation room.

185

The attorney entered with his pen and paper.

"I'm William Wilkens, your assigned lawyer from the Clinton County Legal Aid Society."

"I'm FBI Special Agent John Treehorn. For the record." He didn't budge.

Father Wilkens continued, "I'm also the priest for St. Philomena's Catholic Church in Altona. Do you see this as a conflict with me being a priest and your lawyer?"

David Allen's eyes went from the agent to the attorney.

"No, it's fine. After he leaves, you can explain to me why there may be a problem."

Father Wilkens nodded.

"Can you remove his handcuffs?"

"No," Treehorn answered, "Mr. David Nathan Allen, did FBI Special Agent Melanie Hopper read you your Miranda rights?"

"Yes," David replied.

"Did you make any statement?" Attorney Wilkens asked his client.

"None."

Treehorn's eyes went from the perp to his legal counsel.

"He's handcuffed to the table for the record. We'll be outside if you need us."

The agent shut off the recorder.

"Thank you, Agent Treehorn."

Father Wilkens glared at Thomas outside and then slammed the interrogation room's door.

Treehorn's telephone beeped with a message when he stepped outside.

"I have to take this. I'll be right back."

Melanie observed Treehorn entering an unused interrogation room.

"He had a phone call," Thomas informed her.

As the agent saw the priest she asked, "Is Father Wilkens wearing two hats?"

"That's an example of the joining of the Church and State."

Melanie glanced at the interrogation room occupants who appeared deep in conversation.

Troopers Milner and Holmes stood patiently a few feet away waiting for their next commands.

Melanie whispered to Thomas, "They make a good pair."

Thomas softly spoke, "So do we."

Melanie stepped back before anyone noticed their closeness.

Treehorn called his administrative assistant in his Washington DC office.

"Abby, Treehorn here."

"How's my favorite agent?"

"Missing you. What's up?"

"You received a package today from Altona, NY. It's passed through security."

"When was it sent?"

"Tuesday's postage stamped. Usually agents ask its contents," Abby joked.

Treehorn stated, "It contains a cellphone."

Abby hesitated, "What do I do with it?"

"You have my instructions. Send the cellphone to the Communications Department at Quantico. I'll text Hilda. I'll be in the office on Monday if everything goes as planned."

"You be careful."

"Thanks, Abby."

Treehorn exited the room and waited in the hall with the other LEOs.

Father Wilkens opened the door.

"We're ready for your questions."

Treehorn allowed Melanie to enter the room but blocked Thomas.

"You can watch from the observation room."

Thomas' eyes flashed in anger but he didn't argue.

Treehorn didn't wait to see the man's decision before he entered the interrogation room.

Melanie turned on the video recorder.

"FBI Special Agent Melanie Hopper, present."

"FBI Special Agent John Treehorn."

"William Wilkens, attorney for my client."

"David Nathan Allen. Innocent client."

The perp moved his arm so the handcuffs rattled for the recording.

Treehorn observed the *'Hear No Evil, See No Evil, Speak No Evil'* three monkeys tattoo covering one of his forearms and a cross on his other arm.

"Please reconfirm, Mr. Allen, that your attorney William Wilkens advised you that he is also the priest at St. Philomena's Catholic Church."

"Yes, he did," David spoke.

"Do you wish to have a different lawyer represent you knowing this fact to prevent any conflict?"

"No, we're good," David replied with a nod.

Melanie started, "We're investigating the rape of fourteen-year-old Cate Dixon.

Treehorn tag-teamed, "Your DNA was found on the rape victim."

David looked at his lawyer.

"They planted it."

Melanie countered, "In the fetus in her womb."

"I don't touch jailbait," David argued, showing his first sign of anger.

Wilkens placed his hand on David's cross tattoo.

"Agents, when did the sexual assault occur?"

"Exactly thirteen-and-a-half months ago," Melanie answered.

David smirked as he said, "I told you it wasn't my DNA."

Wilkens and David leaned close and whispered.

"Eighteen months ago, my client was convicted in the State of Kentucky for fourth-degree assault. He served a nine-month sentence. You can check the dates."

Melanie countered, "It's not in his file."

Wilkens and David conferred again.

"Check the name David Nathan," Wilkens recommended.

"His social security number should have matched," Treehorn stated.

"Not if some incompetent clerk typed it in wrong," David complained.

Treehorn's and Melanie's eyes met as they both thought, *Who lied?*

Treehorn changed tactics: "I'm investigating the homicides of Father Bowden, priest at St. Philomena's Catholic Church, and his staff, Loveta Chilton."

"Looking to frame me?"

Wilkens interrupted, "When did the murders occur, for the record?"

"Sunday night, approximately 10pm."

"My client received a speeding ticket in Pennsylvania on Saturday."

Treehorn eyed the pair.

"He could have driven across PA and still have arrived by Sunday evening."

David spat, "Yeah, but those small-town dirty cops didn't like a biker traveling through so they placed me in their rotten jail cell until my appearance in front of the judge on Monday morning."

"We can confirm that story with one telephone call."

Treehorn knew by instinct that the man wasn't lying.

"You do that!" David ordered.

Melanie opened a folder and explained, "DNA doesn't lie. It matched the fetus and the handle of the murder weapon."

David smirked at the female agent as he said, "Your DNA isn't my DNA."

Wilkens turned and eyed the one-way glass. He suspected Thomas stood behind it.

"Is this a new technique for framing innocent citizens?" he questioned.

Treehorn informed the perp, "We have the right to hold you while we verify your story. Do you have a problem with us retesting your DNA?"

Wilkens informed his client, "What the agent is telling you is that the only way you'll be able to leave here is to verify your DNA doesn't match."

David smirked again.

"I have no problem with three hots and a cot until you prove my innocence."

The agents stood, Melanie turned off the recorder, and the pair exited the room making sure the door closed behind them.

Treehorn eyed Troopers Milner and Holmes.

"Send Jimmy down to conduct three DNA tests. Tell him the first stays with this agency but send it to a different State lab, send the second to the University of Arizona, and the third to Quantico. As soon as I'm finished with his paperwork, I want him transported to the county jail."

Troopers Holmes and Milner nodded in agreement.

Melanie confronted Thomas, "You want to tell us how his DNA got switched?"

Thomas' flushed face showed he didn't appreciate the insinuation of impropriety.

Treehorn asked the obvious, "What laboratory processed the DNA on David Allen?"

Thomas accessed the answer on his PDA.

Melanie suggested, "DNA can't be falsified."

"True, but the reports can be," Treehorn offered.

"The files were switched?" Melanie guessed.

"Mr. Allen's DNA wasn't in the database prior to the sexual assault," Treehorn replied with a possible timeline of events.

"So, when the fetus was tested there was no match?" Melanie theorized.

"His name appeared when the lab ran the trace from the murder weapon," Treehorn added.

"The record was then falsified after Cate's suicide, but before the murder," Melanie suggested.

Thomas watched the agents work the summary while he retrieved the information.

Treehorn continued, "The rapist knew Cate was pregnant. He was there when she committed suicide, and that his DNA could and would be traced."

"How did David Allen's DNA get into the database?" Melanie questioned.

"I would say by the same person who removed the rapist's and substituted Mr. Allen's," Treehorn speculated.

Melanie concluded, "It also means the rapist's DNA has been here all along."

Thomas' PDA pinged, "Adirondack Medical Testing Laboratory in Plattsburgh."

He then called his own department, "Jimmy, cross-reference the DNA reports, personnel, and their labs from these two investigations."

Jimmy's voice came across Thomas' speaker, "What am I looking for?"

"Any discrepancies," Thomas ordered.

"Will do," the tech replied.

"Jimmy, work tonight until you have the answers."

"Yes, sir."

Treehorn retrieved the testing laboratory hours.

"They'll be closed before we arrive. Who was the technician listed on Allen's DNA report?"

Thomas searched for the answer, "No name, just tech number 470."

Melanie suggested, "Let's go pay them a visit first thing in the morning."

Treehorn took Thomas aside and said, "Meet me for coffee at 8 am at the Plattsburgh North End Diner."

Thomas glanced at Melanie.

"Alone." It wasn't a request when Treehorn voiced it.

"Understood," Thomas said, meeting the Fed's brown-blue heterochromic eyes without questioning his motive.

"Hopper, we'll meet at the laboratory at 9 am," the senior agent ordered.

"Okay, boss man."

Treehorn walked away without commenting on her flippant attitude.

Chapter Eleven

Theresa McMillan

Treehorn arrived early at the diner after a few hours of sleep and a ten-mile run.

Thomas slid into the booth at exactly 8am dressed not in his New York State Police grey uniform, but a dark suit and tie.

The waitress left two coffees and a carafe then said, "Let me know if you need anything. Name's Brenda Joy. I bring joy to your morning."

Treehorn smiled and said, "Thank you."

Waiting until she was out of earshot he asked Thomas, "How do you think Father Bowden covered up these crimes?" The agent didn't wait for good mornings.

"With help."

"Who specifically?"

"Judge Dooley Stiles," Thomas guessed.

"Why him?"

"They played cards together weekly to pass the time. Who better to instruct the priest on the steps of a criminal investigation than a sitting judge?"

"Maybe," Treehorn replied, but he wasn't buying it.

"Falsifying a DNA report will get you a one-way ticket to jail," Thomas stated the obvious.

"True, but did they know their actions prevented the identification of a rapist?"

"It's still a crime and we'll have our answer soon enough," Thomas stated as he refilled their coffees.

"Tell me about your ex, Tina Dixon."

Treehorn caught the whitening of Thomas' knuckles on his coffee cup handle.

"I've never been married, Agent Treehorn. I literally ran into Tina at a local coffeehouse. We talked, dated, and then lived together. One day I arrived home and she left me a note. Said she accepted a position in Florida. That was the goodbye."

"And Cate?"

"Tina never told me she was eight weeks pregnant at the time. Her medical records after Cate's death confirmed that."

"She never notified you once she gave birth?"

"Nope."

"What was her job?"

"Accountant for an import/export company in Montreal. Their American office is based in Plattsburgh."

"What company?"

"Some big corporation out of New Mexico. They were just a name here: Rathburn Monetary Management."

Treehorn felt a piece of the puzzle fall into place.

"Tell me about her car accident."

"Happened a couple hours southeast of here. North of Elizabethtown. Late at night. Essex County Sheriff's Department came upon the scene. The officer, based on the tire's skid marks, believed she may have swerved to avoid a deer."

"But you questioned it?"

"Not at the time. The sheriff made some observations that someone may have witnessed the accident but nothing conclusive. No one ever came forward to provide a statement."

"I'll visit the site before I leave town."

"His name's in the file."

"Do you have any other questions?"

Treehorn did but he kept them to himself.

"No."

"There's one other thing: Tina never lived in Florida. She moved directly from here to Albuquerque. That's in the record too."

The fax machine assigned to Special Agent Treehorn at the NYS police station activated and printed, "*Birth Record.*" A second sheet followed.

Melanie waited for Treehorn and Thomas in the parking lot of the AMT Lab.

The three entered the dark concrete structure and examined the building's directory.

Treehorn held up his identification to its security, "FBI Special Agents John Treehorn and Melanie Hopper. Official business with Adirondack Medical Testing Laboratory."

"Sign in here," requested the staff, Max. The man then eyed the other male dressed in his suit and asked suspiciously, "Who are you?"

"Captain Thomas Brooks, New York State Police," Thomas stated as he showed his ID.

"Sign in."

"Where's the lab?" Treehorn asked.

"Last door on the right," Max answered as he examined their signatures.

"How many exits are there to that office?"

"Three, the two hallway doors and an emergency exit that's located around the corner. From inside you can see the pair of doors but the rear exit isn't within visual sight of the entrance."

He pointed to a map showing the building's layout; the emergency exit was outlined in red.

Melanie offered, "I'll take the hidden one."

Treehorn pointed to Melanie to take her position.

"The door has a security lock. I'll buzz you in," Max explained.

The officers nodded and entered the secured hallway.

Video surveillance cameras recorded the three LEOs as they walked toward the laboratory.

The door buzzed and Treehorn entered first. Both men found themselves in a glass-protected booth.

A pale, long-bearded lab tech stoner whose age appeared to be near forty ambled to the glass window, where a six-by-six wire opening allowed for conversation.

Treehorn glanced at the man's face and the mug shot on his ID labeled, *Vincent #151.*

"Hey, man, can I help you?"

Presenting his identification Treehorn said, "FBI Special Agent John Treehorn." He didn't mention Thomas. "I need to speak to your supervisor."

Vincent attempted to look authoritative but failed.

"I'm in charge today."

Treehorn pursed his lips and explained, "We need to speak to technician #470."

"Huh?"

Treehorn tapped his chest where Vincent's ID was attached to his pocket.

"Technician #470. Who is it?"

Vincent faced his co-workers and shouted, "Who's 470? The FBI wants you."

The two LEOs watched the staff stop their activity and become spectators.

A woman in a white lab coat stood in a darkened room where a computer monitor glowed. Her eyes didn't rise at the outside commotion; they remained fixed on the screen while she spoke into her cellphone.

Treehorn and Thomas watched her close and lock an office door while still on her cellphone.

"Let us in *now*!" Treehorn shouted.

"Open the door!" Thomas yelled too.

Vincent froze like a deer caught in headlights. Treehorn's fist striking the glass made him jump and press the inner-door release mechanism.

The glass automatically opened and the two officers rushed forward.

Treehorn demanded, "Where is tech #470?"

A young, blond secretary pointed to the darkened room as she said, "Theresa McMillan."

Treehorn tried the knob but found it electronically secured. He looked at the staff and demanded, "Who has an access key? Open it now!"

As Thomas watched Theresa through the room's security glass, he saw her throw something in the trash and then hurry into another room. She glanced up through its small window, meeting Thomas' eyes as she locked the door.

The secretary rushed forward and slid her ID, which doubled as a security card, into the slot. The light turned green and the two men entered with their weapons drawn.

The secretary followed them, sliding her card through a second locking mechanism. This room contained laboratory equipment, chemicals, and a set of glass test tubes.

Treehorn and Thomas secured the area but Theresa was nowhere to be found.

The agent opened the exit door.

Theresa McMillan lay on the ground with her wrists handcuffed behind her and Melanie's knee pressed into her back.

Neither woman said a word.

Treehorn and Melanie each grabbed an arm and assisted the woman off the concrete to a nearby bench. Her photo ID verified her as Theresa McMillan, technician #470. She appeared to be in her late thirties, although she looked older due to her dark, fuzzy hair tied back with a rubber band and the torn clothing she wore beneath her white lab coat.

Thomas addressed Treehorn, "You *need* to see this."

Treehorn ordered Melanie, "Stay here while I check it out."

Thomas handed the agent an evidence bag and pointed to the disposal.

"She trashed her device."

Parts of a cellphone lay scattered in the garbage can. Treehorn took a picture of the pieces in the bin, placed the parts in the evidence bag, and examined it.

"The sim card's missing."

The two men searched the lab.

"Here it is," Thomas said, pointing to an eight-ounce glass container on the shelf; inside liquid bubbled and chemicals disintegrated the card as the pair watched.

Treehorn took out his phone and typed in the chemical formula from the side of the small jar.

"It's safe to transport."

The agent took a picture of the container and placed it in a bag then secured it inside a box.

"I'll have Agent Hopper transport Ms. McMillan back to the station."

Exiting the rear door, they found both women waiting patiently for their return.

"Agent Hopper, transport Theresa in your vehicle. We'll meet you back at the station."

Melanie looked at the object Treehorn held and asked, "What's that?"

"The sim card."

The female agent looked at her detainee and asked incredulously, "Destroying evidence?"

Theresa remained silent.

The door of the laboratory opened and the secretary held out a cheap bag.

"Here's her purse, officer."

"Thanks."

Accepting it, Melanie searched for a weapon. Then she removed Theresa's license and handed it to Treehorn.

He inspected it and pocketed it.

"Let's go. I'll have my communication department pull her phone records."

Melanie loaded Theresa into her SUV and cuffed her wrists to the security bar.

"Mirandize her."

"I did in the hallway."

"Do it again!" Treehorn ordered.

Melanie complied with her partner's request to repeat the legal procedure.

"Theresa McMillan, you have the right to remain silent. Anything you say can and will be used against you in a court of law. You have the right to an attorney. If you cannot afford an attorney, one will be provided for you. Do you understand the rights I have just read to you?"

"Yes," Theresa answered.

"With these rights in mind, do you wish to speak to me?"

"No," came the clipped reply.

Melanie closed her SUV door, glared at her partner, and asked, "Happy *now*?"

Treehorn turned and walked toward his vehicle without commenting.

Melanie felt the urge to poke her partner and yell, "Are you *ever happy*?"

The look he leveled at her made her realize, once again, that she overstepped a line and would pay for it.

Treehorn watched as Melanie's SUV departed the parking lot followed by Thomas'. He quickly completed the communication request and sent it to his department in Quantico with Theresa McMillan's information from her license.

Upon arriving at the State Police precinct, Melanie placed the prisoner in an empty interrogation room.

Theresa McMillan asked as she was being handcuffed to the table, "What crime did I commit?"

"Forgery."

Melanie brought in a landline and told her, "I'll leave you to contact an attorney."

Treehorn watched from the security window. He confirmed the speaker was off as the woman made her one telephone call.

David Allen entered the room followed by Trooper Milner.

Treehorn's head nodded toward Theresa as he asked, "Do you know her?"

The man squinted at the woman through the one-way mirror then replied, "How do you define *know*?"

Treehorn pursed his lips as he frowned.

David smartened up real quick looking at the FBI Agent's displeasure and, considering his circumstance, replied, "I met her at Hank's Hideaway. We spent some time together at a local motel."

"Trooper Milner will transport you to holding while we wait for your DNA results."

"Will she be charged?"

"Yes."

"Agent Treehorn, try to go easy on her if you can. I got the impression she didn't have it easy if you catch my drift."

Trooper Milner opened the door and the two men exited.

Treehorn watched as Melanie entered and removed the landline while Trooper Holmes entered to supervise, as Theresa sat quietly with a haunted look on her face.

Treehorn entered the interrogation room alone and turned on the video recorder.

"I'm FBI Special Agent John Treehorn. Do you wish to waive your rights and speak to us?"

"No. I called my brother. He's asked William Wilkens to support me."

"As your priest or as your attorney?" Treehorn required verbal confirmation.

"Both, and I don't wish to say anything further until he arrives."

Treehorn stated for the record, "Conversation terminated upon request of counsel. If you need anything, Theresa, let Trooper Holmes know."

The agent shut off the recorder and exited the room.

"Did she lawyer up?" Melanie asked what she already knew.

Treehorn informed the two, "No, she *priested* up."

"So, we wait," Melanie stated the obvious.

"I'll stay with you," Thomas flirted.

Melanie caught her partner's lip curl.

"Call me when she's ready to be interviewed," Treehorn said, walking away from the pair.

They watched as the Navajo agent's long legs took him toward the conference room.

"Is he always like that?"

"Yes."

"How did you come to know him?"

Melanie smiled at her memories.

"I was his grasshopper and he was my master."

Thomas' eyebrows rose.

"I met him the day my grandmother put a bullet in a drug dealer's chest. He watched over me as I finished high school and then college. Then he waited at the FBI Academy door for my arrival. The rest is history."

"You love him?"

"No. Treehorn has only allowed his mother and probably one or two others that close. The rest of us admire him for his dedication and drive. He seeks justice every day for his victims."

"What mistake does a criminal make with him?"

"They assume his silence is a weakness. They don't realize that he never, ever, forgets the details of an investigation regardless of how small or insignificant."

Thomas looked at the empty hallway.

"I'll remember that. He doesn't seem too focused on Father Bowden's or Loveta Chilton's murders."

Melanie chuckled as she walked away.

"Then you've assumed wrong."

Thomas once again examined the *Lady Justice* mural in the hallway as he waited for the lawyer's arrival.

"Does she provide a moral reckoning for you?" Father Wilkens asked as he arrived carrying his briefcase.

"No, but then how honorable are you when a sinner rings the *devil's doorbell* on the confessional booth and tells you of the crimes they committed? You absolve them without penalty!"

"It's my job and it's better than your type of justice."

"Are you here in the name of the Church or the State?" Thomas asked facetiously, "Are you here to hide Miss McMillan's illegal activity in the name of your God?"

"It appears both this time."

"One of these days that collar of yours will trip you up," Thomas gave his opinion.

Father Wilkens frowned as he responded, "I very much doubt that."

"Theresa's in Interrogation Room #1. We'll be waiting outside for her confession."

The lawyer walked away, effectively ending their conversation.

"No electronic devices in the room. Trooper Holmes will watch your briefcase for you and I'll let the Feds know you've arrived."

The lawyer knocked on the door and entered with his belongings to spite Thomas.

Trooper Holmes immediately stepped out carrying the attorney's briefcase.

Thomas smirked as he notified the Special Agents.

The agents waited patiently outside until Father Wilkens opened the door.

"We're ready for you now."

Thomas started for the door but Treehorn stopped him.

"Stay outside."

The captain wanted to argue but realized his presence could compromise his daughter's investigation. Grabbing Treehorn's arm he whispered, "Ask her if she's connected to Judge Stiles, Gardenia Myers, or Joseph Granger."

Treehorn nodded once to acknowledge that he heard this.

As the Special Agents followed Father Wilkens into the interrogation room, Treehorn immediately pressed the record button.

"FBI Special Agent John Treehorn."

"FBI Special Agent Melanie Hopper. Please identify yourselves," she requested.

"Father William Wilkens, priest at St. Philomena's Catholic Church in Altona, New York."

"Theresa McMillan."

Treehorn verified, "Have your Miranda rights been read to you, Ms. McMillan?"

"Yes."

"Do you feel there is a conflict of interest that Father Wilkens is representing you both as an attorney and as a priest?"

"No," Theresa firmly replied.

Treehorn eyed the woman who appeared older than her thirty-five years of age. The special agent knew the rape case and murder cases were intertwined. He now wondered whether this woman held the key that would unlock their secrets.

"Do you know Judge Dooley Stiles?" Treehorn asked.

Melanie's raised eyebrows showed surprise at Treehorn's question.

"He's my godfather."

"What about Gardenia Myers?"

"I stayed with her for a couple of years when I was a teenager."

Treehorn took a professional look at the woman's face, hair color, eyes, and bone structure before adding, "What about Joseph Granger?"

Father Wilkens leaned forward as if he wanted to interrupt but instead remained silent.

"The guy who runs the greasy spoon diner?" Theresa asked without meeting Treehorn's eyes.

"Yes."

"I could recognize him on the street."

The agent squinted at her answer.

Melanie took a different approach by asking, "Are you adopted?" The agent wondered if she was the girl Eleanor Humphrey surrendered for adoption all those years ago?

"What?" Eyeing Father Wilkens, Theresa received her answer, "Oh my God!"

"The church maintains many confidences," the priest stressed.

Theresa's face paled.

"I feel ill."

"Was it a church adoption?" Melanie drove home the point as she handed the garbage can to Theresa in perfect timing.

"I'm going to be sick."

The shackle limited the woman's movement as she puked.

Treehorn unlocked the handcuffs, handed her his crisp white handkerchief, and ordered Melanie, "Get her a fresh pail and a glass of water."

The agent returned a minute later with both.

Theresa's hand shook as she tried to sip the liquid.

"Do you want to know what my life has been like?"

"You don't have to answer their questions," Father Wilkens informed her.

She turned on him shouting, "Church adoption? Who are my parents?"

"We're waiting for verification," Treehorn answered, "Unless Father Wilkens would like to disclose their identity?"

"I'm not at liberty," the two-hatted man replied.

The woman sneered, "Of course not!"

Treehorn sympathized, "Tell me about your life."

"Father Bowden visited me every year on my birthday. My parents argued about it. I never knew he brought money and I was never told that I was adopted."

Tears rolled down her face.

"My mom died of cancer when I was thirteen. That's when my nightmare began."

She huddled deeper into her tattered sweater as if trying to block out the painful memories.

"The man I thought was my father told me one night when he entered my room that he wasn't."

No one interrupted her.

"He told Father Bowden to stop coming but to keep sending the cash. What was the money for?" She looked up at Father Wilkens for the answer.

"I don't know," he replied.

"You're lying!"

She bowed her head and cried.

"I ran away when I was sixteen because the man couldn't keep his hands off me. Do you understand?"

Her eyes showed the realization. The priest tried to comfort the abused victim.

"Father Bowden located me. I never told him what had happened but I think he knew."

"Is that when you lived with Gardenia Myers?"

"Yes, I stayed there until I went to college. The priest paid for my education and refused my offers to repay him."

Treehorn observed Theresa's now-composed face as he asked, "How long have you worked at the laboratory?"

"Almost five years."

"How did you know David Nathan Allen?"

"We dated a few times."

Theresa avoided Treehorn's eye contact, again.

"Did you change the record in your laboratory database using Mr. Allen's DNA?"

Father Wilkens interrupted, "Don't answer that! Whoever did... committed a crime."

"Whose name should be on the record?" Treehorn demanded.

The priest, now definitely a lawyer, placed his hand on Theresa's arm.

"Don't answer any of their questions."

Theresa followed his instructions and stayed silent.

Treehorn continued, "You didn't know Pennsylvania updated their DNA database to include misdemeanors?"

Melanie tag-teamed, "David Allen had a record in Pennsylvania. Whose name should be on the record?"

Father Wilkens ordered. "Stay silent, Theresa!"

"Who asked you to falsify a DNA record?"

"She's not answering that," the priest informed the agents.

Theresa followed her lawyer's advice.

Treehorn grilled, "Why deny it when we have proof?"

Theresa looked at her lawyer and then at the FBI agents before requesting, "I'd like to

speak to my attorney alone for a minute. Is that possible?"

Treehorn nodded and turned off the video recorder. The agents exited the room.

Melanie suggested, "She may want a plea deal."

"She got caught," Treehorn explained, confronting his co-worker, *"Buddha said three things cannot be long hidden: the sun, the moon, and the truth."*

Chapter Twelve

Two Tales

Stella approached the agents and handed Treehorn two documents.

"Thank you, Mrs. Hunter," the Special Agent said.

Reading the first document, he handed it to Melanie.

"Eleanor Humphrey gave birth to a daughter. No name is listed for the father or child."

"Theresa," Melanie speculated.

Treehorn read the second document and then thrust it into Melanie's hand.

"Miss Humphrey had twins."

Melanie examined the birth certificates. A girl and a boy. Then she remembered the faded marks on Eleanor's living room wall.

"When I visited her, two pictures had been removed. They may have been photos of her two children."

Treehorn and Melanie entered the room and turned on the video recorder.

"Theresa is refusing to answer any more questions at this time."

"Then she can listen," Treehorn responded.

Melanie glanced over to the one-way glass where Thomas watched from the other side. Then she accessed the DMV records.

"Who asked you to switch the name on the DNA record?" Treehorn asked, slamming the woman's birth certificate down on the table.

Theresa touched it as if it were something precious. Her eyes drawn to the *Name* line where it listed only *'Girl - Humphrey'*.

"How did you obtain those records?" Father Wilkens demanded.

"Why? Is there more than one?" Treehorn nailed the priest with his plural mistake, "Are you representing the Church or your client with that question?"

Theresa interrupted the men with a whisper, "Eleanor Humphrey. She's Gardenia Myers' sister. I lived with my aunt for two years and never once did she tell me that we were related." Her lips quivered as her face paled, "What kind of person does that?"

"Is this your date of birth?" Melanie confirmed the woman's data on her driver's license.

Theresa examined it and gave a brief nod.

"She's your mother."

"Is she still alive?"

Melanie replied, "Yes."

The agent didn't inform her that she met with the woman the previous day.

Theresa looked to her right at the priest and asked sadly, "Another confidence?"

Then, her eyes swung to Treehorn as he held a second document.

"Whose report did you switch?" the agent grilled.

"You already know."

Treehorn handed Theresa the second birth certificate.

"Your twin brother."

Theresa didn't look surprised in the least.

"Father Bowden told me he needed a name changed on a DNA report because he owed a judge a favor." She wiped her eyes with a tissue. "After I changed the name, I realized the record matched my date of birth. The priest said that I owed him."

Treehorn demanded, "What's his name?" as his phone pinged.

Melanie asked in a calmer voice, "Who is he?"

Theresa smirked at both agents as she said, "A no-name birth certificate."

Treehorn leaned into the woman's space and said, "When I match his date of birth, then I'll have his identity."

Theresa remained silent and detached.

"Let me speak to my client," Father Wilkens respectfully requested.

Treehorn examined his telephone.

"We no longer need your cooperation. Your brother raped a fourteen-year-old teen. She committed suicide when her pregnancy results tested positive."

Theresa's shocked expression showed she knew the horror that had been forcefully inflicted.

Father Wilkens shouted, "That was unnecessary!"

Treehorn slammed his hand down on the table and pointed at the priest.

"Why don't you ask *him?* Who's your daddy?"

"I'm filing a complaint against you with your agency."

"Go right ahead. I'll give you their address."

Treehorn eyed the two with contempt and exited the room.

Melanie shut off the recorder and followed him out into the hallway.

"Wasn't that a little harsh?" she confronted him as they heard the woman's scream.

Treehorn snarled at his partner, "Confessions of a dead priest."

Melanie pursed her lips and kept her mouth shut as she waited for her next order.

"You two, finish processing her booking. I'll be in the conference room with Jimmy."

Treehorn glanced at the female officers and walked away.

Trooper Holmes' eyes rounded.

"I'd hate to be near him if he lost it."

"See his bruises? That's him losing it."

Thomas joined the women when he exited the observation room.

Melanie offered her sympathy to him, "I'm sorry they sabotaged the investigation."

"That's what criminals do, Agent Hopper."

Trooper Holmes added, "They all get what's coming to them in the end."

Thomas and Melanie looked at each other. They each had their own thoughts on the matter, but kept it to themselves.

Jimmy waited patiently for Treehorn's arrival.

"What did you find?" the agent asked as soon as he entered the room.

"Ms. McMillan's tampered record belongs to..." the technician stepped aside as his two hands pointed toward the bulletin board. The enlarged DMV photos of Theresa and her brother were pinned next to each other. "…Joseph Granger."

Jimmy gave two thumbs up.

Thomas heard the revelation as he entered and saw the exhibit.

Treehorn re-examined the twins' birth certificates and their matching dates of birth on their government-issued documents and driver's licenses.

"Twins. Look at the resemblance."

"The DNA results came back from the knife. Four samples found on it. Father Bowden's paternal DNA, a maternal, and their male and female offspring."

"The knife was used to cut their umbilical cords."

"The kids were adopted by two different families," Thomas added.

"Father Bowden kept in contact with Theresa. We know that he and Joseph provided each other an alibi the night Cate committed suicide. Now, we know who raped your daughter," Treehorn stated the facts.

Thomas continued, "Father Bowden covered it up. He knew his son committed the crime."

Treehorn added, "Joseph witnessed your daughter take her life. He recognized the gun, which was probably the same weapon the priest gave to Cate to protect her from his own flesh and blood."

"The same gun that killed Father Bowden and Loveta Chilton."

"You stared at a rapist for a year," Treehorn pressed.

"You stared at a murderer for a week," Thomas' face flushed.

"You may want to believe Joseph killed his father and housekeeper but we don't have proof."

Treehorn gave Thomas a very long look that was interrupted by the ringing telephone.

"Special Agent John Treehorn."

"Frank Diaz from Communications. I have McMillan's telephone calls from Plattsburgh. She telephoned Joseph Granger and then the St. Philomena's Catholic Church Rectory."

"Thank you. Email me the report."

Relaying the information to Thomas he said, "She called Joseph and the rectory. Put out an APB on Granger. He'll be on the run."

"Father Bowden and Judge Stiles protected the man even though they knew he raped a teenager," Thomas roared, slamming his fist down on the table.

Treehorn ignored the man's outburst as he examined the laboratory results on the bulletin board.

"He volunteered his DNA to rule himself out as the perpetrator because he knew Theresa would falsify the name on the report."

"DNA eliminated him and fingered him," Thomas added, grabbing his jacket.

"Let's get him!" Treehorn ordered.

The Federal agents and State Police, dressed in black fatigues and fully weaponized, poured out of the building and climbed into their unmarked black and blue SUVs.

Treehorn looked at Thomas in his rearview mirror.

"I don't need to tell you to stay behind me and let me do my job."

Melanie glanced at Thomas.

"I understand," the captain replied for the record.

Treehorn repeated an important clue from early in the investigation.

"The priest received a telephone call before he died. He said, *'I did a terrible thing. I lied for you once, never again!'*"

"Had to be Joseph," Thomas speculated.

"The priest lied about his son's alibi the night Cate died."

"You think Joseph was at Cate's suicide?" Melanie asked.

"Yes. I'm guessing he removed the gun."

"Then how did that weapon come to kill Father Bowden and Loveta Chilton?" she questioned, "He had no reason to leave it at the scene of the crime."

Treehorn glanced in his rearview mirror.

"Unless the killer wanted it left there for a reason."

The Special Agent's SUV led the convoy of police vehicles that crept into town without their lights or sirens activated.

They stopped a short distance from the diner.

The LEOs took the time to check their weapons.

Treehorn checked his Glock and stated the one thing he had silently questioned since the beginning of the investigation, "The gun connects the crimes, but it doesn't prove that Joseph killed his father or the housekeeper."

Melanie wondered why Treehorn kept his focus on that aspect of the investigation.

"Why would he wait a year to kill his father?" she asked, checking her second weapon.

Thomas suggested a motive, "The coroner said Father Bowden suffered mini-strokes and that he pointed out the sinners of his community."

"Do you think his deteriorating health could have caused him to expose all of them?" Melanie suggested.

"The killer may have thought that," Treehorn surmised.

"Or maybe Father Bowden had other secrets. We're assuming everything is related to Joseph Granger's crime. What if it was something totally different?" Thomas theorized.

"It would have had to be important enough to provide a motive for murder," Melanie pointed to the obvious.

Treehorn eyed Thomas in his rearview mirror.

"We can ask Joseph when we arrest him."

Thomas met Treehorn's eyes as he replied, "Yes, we can."

"Cate's assault case would never have been solved without Bowden's murder," Melanie deduced.

"I know," Thomas said, realizing the same.

Treehorn scoped out the area. The diner, the foster care home next door where Cate committed suicide, the church on the other side, and the rectory behind it. Three of the four structures whose residents set up, perpetrated, and then covered up a horrible crime against a minor.

An automobile matching the suspect's car sat next to the closed diner.

Treehorn used his FBI computer to verify ownership of the vehicle. A second later information appeared on the screen: "It's Granger's car."

"It's common knowledge that Joseph lives above the diner," Thomas said, eyeing the establishment.

Treehorn looked at the locations of the other officers as they exited their vehicles, spread out, and surrounded the building.

Treehorn pounded on the door shouting, "FBI! Joseph Granger, we have an arrest warrant."

Silence.

A state trooper held a door ram.

Treehorn shook his head, stepped back, and kicked in the door on his first attempt.

The officers entered the foyer and progressed up the stairs in a standard search formation.

"All clear," the police spoke as they checked the rooms and then holstered their weapons.

Clothes covered the furniture and floor, while dirty dishes lined the counter.

"Ew, what a slob!" Melanie said, scrunching up her nose.

The Crime Scene Unit technicians entered carrying their equipment.

Treehorn and Thomas looked out the perp's window located above his pillow. It had a direct line to Cate's bedroom at the foster care home. The two men's eyes met and for a split second they understood each other and why they wore gold badges.

CSU staff member Eileen Fulton handed Melanie a shoebox.

"It contains photos of Cate Dixon. I worked her case."

"Thanks."

The agent used her pen to examine them and handed it to her partner.

"What's inside? Treehorn's eyebrow raised.

"Pictures of Cate."

Thomas came forward to examine the images. The photos showed her smiling with a couple of girlfriends.

Some pictures had Cate circled in red ink and other people in the photos X'd out.

Treehorn assessed, "He stalked her."

"Looks that way," Melanie agreed.

She handed the box back to Eileen.

Treehorn observed the blinking light on the answering machine and pressed the 'play' button.

Theresa McMillan's voice, "The police are here. They know what I did. *Run!*"

"That's one message he shouldn't have missed," Melanie said, her flippant attitude returning.

"So, where is he?" Noticing that the rectory lights were on Treehorn added, "Hooper and Holmes. See if the priest has company at the rectory."

Two State Troopers in SWAT clothing added, "We'll stay here and wait for his return."

Trooper Milner added, "I'll grab a rover and patrol the area."

Treehorn moved his head toward the stone structure.

"You and I will check the church," he said to Thomas.

Thomas looked at the glowing stained glass windows of St. Philomena's Catholic Church and activated his mouthpiece, "Everyone canvas your assigned areas. Suspect has not been located."

The Fed ordered, "Let's find him!"

Treehorn and Thomas prowled toward the church with their weapons drawn, each with their own agenda.

The agent looked at the large, imposing building in the fading light as he climbed its granite steps. The hairs stood up on the back of his neck. He knew there was a threat here and he wondered who it would appear from.

"I'll take the front entrance. You take the rear."

Both men entered the church in full law enforcement safety mode and met in the middle at the altar.

"I'll check the rooms on this side," the agent spoke softly.

Thomas pointed to the confessionals, restrooms, and storage area. Silence greeted him as he searched the baptismal vestibule. This time his reflection appeared clear in its water.

Treehorn continued to search the empty offices. Joseph Granger was nowhere to be found.

Meanwhile, Thomas slowly approached the confessional booths.

Father Wilkens waited for him, dressed in his black robes with its standard white collar. A well-used bible held in his joined hands.

"Thomas."

"Father," the captain said, lowering his gun.

The priest pointed to the confessional booth and whispered, "I want you to repent."

"Not going to happen."

The officer searched the confessionals with his raised gun. He pressed his finger against the ringer on the booth.

"I call this the *devil's doorbell*. They come and speak with a forked tongue, telling you lies and deceit."

The priest whispered, "I'm going to inform the police of your confession."

"That's good because I'm not admitting it again. Where is he?"

"Who?"

"Did you promise Joseph asylum here?"

"No."

"First smart thing you've done. Is he in the rectory?"

Father Wilkens stayed silent.

Agent Hopper and Trooper Holmes entered the rectory with their weapons drawn as they quietly searched the premises.

A light illuminated an upstairs bedroom.

They announced their arrival, "Police!"

The woman screamed when they spoke. The clean linen fell from her hands as she raised them and pleaded, "Don't shoot!"

"FBI. Who are you?" Melanie asked the young brunette.

"Megan O'Neil. I'm the new housekeeper."

"Are you the only person here?"

"Yes."

"Where's Father Wilkens?"

"He's at the church."

"Is he alone?"

"No, Joseph Granger's with him."

The LEOs looked at each other and rushed to the church.

"Where's Joseph Granger?" Treehorn grilled the priest after he finished his search and found him with Thomas.

"I won't have you killing..." Father Wilkens stopped.

Treehorn's eyes shifted from man to man as an implication emerged.

Neither man chose to finish the sentence.

A shifting shadow through the stained glass caught the agent's eye at the same time the church bells began to ring, causing white pigeons to fly from its steeple.

"Stay and wait here in case he escapes."

Thomas nodded.

"Don't sabotage this investigation," the Fed said assertively to Thomas and the priest.

"We understand, Agent Treehorn," Father Wilkens answered for both of them.

Treehorn stated to Thomas, matter-of-factly, "It would be a shame if a stray bullet struck you if you disobeyed my order, right?"

Father Wilkens' eyes rounded as the bells finished their tune. He realized he had underestimated the FBI agent.

Thomas wasn't given an opportunity to comment.

Treehorn put his finger to his lips, pointed upward, and turned toward the stairs.

Thomas assessed the situation, his options, and whispered to the priest, "If you don't tell me where he's hiding, I'm going to shoot him when I find him."

Father Wilkens bowed his head and pointed to the church belfry.

"Please don't kill him."

"I can't promise that. Stay here and tell the others where we're located."

Thomas followed the agent up the stairs of the tall square tower, hoping the Fed wouldn't shoot him for disobeying his direct order.

Treehorn continued up the perimeter wooden staircase on his hunt for the assailant. More pigeons flew from their outside perch, as the agent continued his climb above the bell to the landing that reminded him of the window walk on his father's beachfront retreat.

Thomas found the agent as he passed a solid wall support to the open tower.

Treehorn shouted, "Joseph Granger, FBI. Come out with your hands up!"

The criminal stood on the edge of the window walk with a thin rope tied around his neck.

"Stop or I'll jump!"

Treehorn and Thomas aimed their weapons at the man since he kept one hand hidden behind his back.

"I'll do it!" Granger threatened.

Thomas clearly stated, "Do it."

"Show us your hands and remove the rope," Treehorn countered.

Joseph shuffled his feet, "I'll do it."

Thomas, father of Cate, showed his lack of morals under the circumstances by saying, "Do it. You'll save the taxpayers a prison bill."

"Back off, *now!*"

Treehorn's terse order didn't stop Thomas as he casually took a step closer to Joseph and asked, "Could you answer a couple of questions before you jump?"

"Stay back!"

Joseph's face developed a fine sheen.

Thomas continued for Treehorn's benefit as the lead investigator, or maybe it was just an engrained law enforcement officer's never-ending need to question a criminal's motivation, "Cate Dixon. Why did you assault her?"

Joseph smiled. The type of salacious grin that makes a police officer willingly put a bullet in a perp.

"She was special. I watched her every night from my bedroom window."

Thomas requested as the girl's father, "I want you to jump."

"I couldn't help myself," Joseph whispered as he showed his hands. "She tasted like cake."

Treehorn took another step toward the offender.

"I knew my DNA would be traced to the baby."

Treehorn stopped and listened.

"My father and I argued about her. I threatened to reveal his dirty secrets if he exposed mine."

Treehorn asked one question that only this man could finally answer, "Were you with her the night she committed suicide?"

Joseph nodded as his face flushed in anger.

"I recognized the gun. I realized my father must have given it to her to use against me."

"Then what happened?" Treehorn listened as the man continued his confession.

"I took the gun," Joseph said with a smirk, "I returned it to my father. We argued. Then, I told him she was pregnant and that she used it to kill herself. What you don't know is Gardenia Myers and Dooley Stiles blackmailed me. She watched from the window to keep me quiet while the judge listened as I told him what I did to the girl."

Waving his weapon from Joseph's face to the rope, Treehorn ordered, "Get down! I'm taking you in."

As Joseph moved away from Treehorn but closer to the edge he said, "I wanted my father to know he caused her death with his gun."

Treehorn stated in a clear and concise voice, "No, you caused it."

"I was his son."

"She was your victim."

Treehorn stepped closer to Joseph.

"You're under arrest for the rape of Cate Dixon."

The slamming of doors echoed upward.

Thomas added, "I'm arresting you for the murder of your father and Loveta Chilton."

Treehorn remained silent on that statement as sirens could be heard approaching.

Joseph panicked, "I didn't kill him and you can't prove it!"

Thomas continued without Treehorn's approval, "You will be given a trial. You can explain how you removed the gun from a suicide and then used it to commit two homicides."

"You can't frame me for that!"

Joseph didn't want to spend the rest of his pathetic life in prison.

Treehorn ordered the officer, "Shut up!"

Thomas didn't surrender his anger.

"Ballistics proved the bullets are from the same gun. You're going down."

The police vehicles stopped outside the building as Joseph jumped.

Treehorn rushed forward.

Thomas didn't move but stood fixated on the suffering man.

Treehorn looked over the railing.

The whites of Joseph's eyes shone as he grabbed the rope above the noose in an attempt to relieve the tightness; as the panic set in, he swung his legs in the air to find anything to anchor himself on.

Thomas holstered his weapon and watched as the rope swayed left to right like a pendulum that swung the time of justice.

"Let him hang," he said without a bit of remorse.

Treehorn looked at his watch, the one his father gave him the day he graduated from the FBI Academy.

Fidelity, Bravery, and Integrity.

He raised his pistol, aimed, and pulled its trigger. The bullet struck the rope and then ricocheted off a church bell as one bundle of stranded hemp began to unravel.

Father Wilkens, Melanie, and Trooper Holmes heard the gunshot.

Joseph grabbed the rope above his neck which gave him one lung full of air.

Thomas ran down the stairs as Treehorn aimed a second shot at the swinging rope. Its projectile sliced the rope as the second gunfire reverberated throughout the church.

Joseph's body dropped and slammed against another bronze bell. His arms flayed in the wind trying to grab anything that would stop or slow his descent to the floor below.

Treehorn confirmed the man was free from his hanging.

Joseph fell past Thomas as the officer rushed down the stairs. Treehorn holstered his weapon and ran for the stairs.

Joseph slammed against the floor followed by the rope still connected to his neck.

Thomas' boots pounded down the last few steps.

Joseph struggled to rise in an attempt to escape.

"Let me help you!" the priest pleaded with the criminal.

Melanie rushed forward with her gun drawn.

"Get away from him, Father!"

The priest stepped in front of the agent and assisted the man up from the floor.

Joseph grabbed him like a life preserver begging, "He's crazy. You gotta help me!"

"You need to stop what you're doing and repent."

Joseph looked at the priest as if he too was his enemy.

"You're as bad as my father was."

Thomas stepped toward the two men.

"Get back, Father!"

As Joseph pulled a knife on the priest, Treehorn exited the tower.

"All of you, get back."

Melanie and Trooper Holmes complied with his order.

"Don't make this any harder on yourself," Father Wilkens pleaded.

Joseph pointed the knife at Thomas and snapped, "He wants to charge me with murder. I didn't kill my father."

Treehorn and Thomas watched, waiting for their next move.

The priest acknowledged, "I know you didn't. You need to drop the weapon or these officers will do their job."

"How do you know he didn't kill his father?" Treehorn asked.

Father Wilkens opened his mouth to answer but Thomas interrupted, "Put down the weapon, Joseph, or I'm going to shoot you!"

Treehorn clenched his weapon until his knuckles turned white.

Joseph tightened his grip around the priest's neck.

242

"I admit I raped the girl but I swear inside these walls that I didn't kill my father."

Melanie and Trooper Holmes waited for the conflict to end.

Father Wilkens saw Thomas' intent to fire his weapon.

Joseph cried out, "She kept her window open so I wouldn't turn my eyes towards any other young girl. I can still hear her screams."

The priest moved in front of Thomas' gun to block his intended shot.

Treehorn's gun exploded with one shot at the rapist.

Joseph dropped to the floor screaming with a shattered femur as his knife slid across the tiled floor.

Father Wilkens' horrified look at the outcome didn't affect anyone.

Thomas holstered his weapon followed by the agent.

Treehorn stepped up to the priest and advised him, "Never get between a bullet and a felon!"

Father Wilkens replied, "I'll try to remember that in both of my professions."

Treehorn offered to Thomas, "You can do the honors of handcuffing him."

The captain reached for his cuffs before the agent finished his sentence.

Treehorn continued, "Read him his rights, Agent Hopper, and have Trooper Holmes witness it."

Melanie nodded and watched as her partner walked away.

The women officers administered first aid to Joseph and guarded him as they waited for the EMS personnel to arrive.

No one could stop his agonized cries for help.

Thomas observed the rapist.

Treehorn watched the murderer.

One man handcuffed while the other one was free.

Treehorn stood back and watched, silently and no one dared to disturb him.

Chapter Thirteen

Justified

Police cars, the Crime Scene Unit vehicle, and emergency personnel surrounded the premises.

An exhausted Thomas walked out of the church and leaned against Treehorn's SUV. He stared off towards the cemetery where his daughter's body rested.

Father Wilkens found him there. "Are you okay?"

Thomas didn't answer as the two men watched the police activity.

"I don't think he'll walk a straight line again, but then, did he ever?"

"You know he's not a murderer." Father Wilkens admitted.

"Father Bowden and Betty Luzer were the only people who knew about the gun and diary. They're not here to discuss it." Thomas wasn't feeling sympathetic to the cause.

"You're framing an innocent man for murder."

Thomas countered, "Isn't my daughter's life worth something?"

The priest shook his head at the law-enforcement officer.

"Don't worry about the murder charge. He'll be lucky to survive his stint in state prison for rape."

The priest prayed for this man's soul. "Is that why you didn't kill him?"

"I know Joseph will suffer, because no inmate likes a sexual predator." Thomas curled his lips and whispered. "And here I thought Agent Treehorn would nail me for murder."

"Someone has to. May God have mercy on your soul, and Josephs'."

The men watched a handcuffed and bandaged assailant pushed on a gurney from the church to the ambulance. The doors of the emergency vehicle slammed shut and departed with its lights and sirens blaring. Two New York State Police vehicles followed it.

Melanie and Troopers Holmes and Milner approached the men.

Agent Hopper the captain, "Congratulations, you got your man."

Thomas eyed the trio. "We got him." He then ordered his two officers, "Would you take Father Wilkens inside and have him write his statement?"

The priest stared at Thomas, "We'll continue this conversation another day."

Father Wilkens and the two Troopers walked away.

"You've trained them well." Melanie's PDA beeped and she read the message. "They're transporting the others to the station."

Treehorn watched as a NYSP blue-and-gold patrol car drove by. Dooley Stiles and Gardenia Myers sat handcuffed in the rear seat."

CSU Harris approached him with his evidence collection kit.

Treehorn ordered, "I want you to check for DNA and fingerprints on all of the exterior windows at the diner and Cate Dixon's window from when she committed suicide. Cross reference them to Gardenia Myers."

"Yes, sir." Harris approved.

Melanie added, "Won't look too good when the town historian becomes exposed as a voyeur."

"She is what she is." Treehorn stated as he supervised the crime scene.

A short time later, the agent's busy in the conference room packing up all of the investigation materials related to

247

his case. He took special care with every item removed from the bulletin board.

Stella Hunter entered. "Agent Treehorn, here's Tina Dixon's accident report along with her employment records. I found it odd that there's no employment history with her social security number after leaving Plattsburgh."

"Thank you Mrs. Hunter."

"It's been a pleasure working with you and I hope you have a safe journey home."

"Thanks."

Stella leaned forward and whispered something in his ear.

Treehorn responded, "I know."

Stella smiled. Those types of facial movements that tell a story and its conclusion.

The agents watched her leave.

"What did she whisper?"

Treehorn ignored the question so Melanie asked another.

"Why pull Tina Dixon's records?"

"Tell me again how you made Special Agent Hopper?"

"You recommended me?"

"Yes, but only after you screwed up by giving Shady Lynch a favor."

"I made a mistake."

"Exactly. Learn. I don't leave any stone unturned. Did you happen to ask Thomas why, after all these years, Tina was returning to him?"

"The daughter may have wanted to meet her father."

"And you think they had to drive from New Mexico to New York to accomplish that?"

"Not with social media."

"When you're having dinner with Thomas tonight, why don't you ask him what his thoughts are on the matter." He sarcastically stated.

Melanie didn't respond but instead helped Treehorn finish packing the boxes.

Once all of the evidence was secured in his vehicle, he ordered Melanie, "Go join the party."

"Where will you be?"

"At the hotel, working." Treehorn raised his eyebrow. The one that the catgut stitch no longer held.

"Have fun!" She flippantly replied as she walked away.

Treehorn spoke to her back, "Do you know what the State Police motto is? *Excellence Through Knowledge.* Remember that Special Agent Hopper."

She turned and watched her partner drive away, knowing she missed an opportunity.

Melanie joined the party as Major Morgan, in full dress uniform, cut a cake that held the New York State Police logo on it. Sure enough, their motto that Treehorn stated was printed in frosting beneath it.

Thomas greeted Melanie as she entered. He asked about her partner, then let her mingle.

Everyone celebrated the justice that had finally arrived for one of their own.

Thomas watched Melanie as she visited with Troopers Holmes and Milner while the caterers kept busy delivering appetizers and drinks to his staff.

Major Morgan and Thomas raised their drinks to the three officers who returned their salute.

"I'm giving Holmes and Milner merit awards. They didn't catch the killer but did a fine job in the investigation. You can tell the governor that Granger confessed to the rape of my daughter."

"Any status on the murders?"

"Granger denied killing them but admitted taking possession of the murder weapon." Thomas's half-truths flowed like church wine.

"Send me the report. Anything else?"

"I have a dirty judge who needs to be removed from office."

"Send me the information and you can consider it done."

Thomas smirked. Power had its privilege.

Major Morgan whispered to Thomas, "I'm putting you in for a promotion."

"I don't want one."

"What do you want?"

"I've decided to take you up on your offer."

"Which one? I've offered you many over the years."

"Cold case division."

"Good choice. They could use your level of expertise."

"I feel the area has a lot to offer."

Major Morgan eyed his professional staff, "Where's Agent Treehorn?"

"His partner said he returned to the hotel to work."

"The murders?"

"Who knows?"

Treehorn texted Raven, *"I'm missing the Land of my People."*

Raven responded, *"You should visit soon."*

Treehorn went to the hotel lobby landline and used his prepaid credit card to telephone Raven's burner phone, "Hello my friend. What did you find?"

"Did you catch the bad guy?"

"I'm working on it."

"I sent you a secured email with all of the details. Password is your favorite criminal: Rathburn." Raven joked. "Here's the details and what Mancuso may know."

Treehorn listened and thanked his fellow agent.

Dr. Mario Mancini entered his office on Saturday morning to catch up on paperwork and see two patients. When he opened the newspaper the headline stated, *"ALTONA RESIDENT ARRESTED FOR SEXUAL ASSAULT OF TEEN" Joseph Granger, Altona, was arrested by the New York State Police for the sexual assault of fourteen-year-old Cate Dixon..."* The psychiatrist finished the story and hoped it would bring some closure to Thomas but he doubted it.

Upon finishing the paper, the doctor started on his pile of mail. He found a letter addressed to him from the NYS Police.

> *Dear Dr. Mancini,*
> *I'm no longer in need of your services.*
> *—Captain Thomas Brooks*

Dr. Mancini frowned.

Treehorn drove to his meeting with the Essex County Sheriff deputy. The law enforcement agency that investigated Tina Dixon's fatal car crash was located in Elizabethtown, New York. Treehorn examined the map and wondered if Altona was, in fact, her destination the night of the fatal accident or another location.

Sergeant Tom Peralta met him upon his arrival. A sharp, thirty-something officer with bright, blue eyes and a short buzz cut. His backbone showed a military bearing. After introductions, they addressed the issue at hand.

"Tina Dixon."

Sgt. Peralta pointed to two evidence boxes and two tagged suitcases. "This were the contents of her car. One other suitcase went with the girl."

Treehorn frowned at the lot.

"I tracked down the ex-husband in Albuquerque. Here's the address."

Treehorn glanced at the paper and then set it aside.

"So, I sent the local police to the residence for some background information. The house was being vacated. Everything being donated immediately to a local charity."

"He emptied their house of her belongings. No crime there." Treehorn knew families conducted themselves strangely upon death and traumatic events. He also realized from the investigation that Tina kept secrets.

The deputy shook his head. "Mr. Dixon met the officer. He informed him that *'his wife'* had fled with her daughter and allegedly left a note that stated she would be filing for a divorce. He stated he didn't want anything to do with the daughter and considered the matter closed."

"Standup guy." Treehorn's sarcasm wasn't lost on the deputy.

"The officer felt the man's actions appeared odd, so he returned to the house later to check on it."

"What did he find?"

"Absolutely nothing. Every room had been emptied right down to the bare floors."

"Okay." Treehorn squinted and waited, patiently.

"I asked the officer to do a background check on Kyle Dixon. Here's what he found."

Treehorn examined the basic information.

"Mr. Dixon, a security consultant, was happily married and living with his wife in a separate house. He'd never been married to this woman. A ruse."

Treehorn knew Tina had created an elaborate fake identification upon leaving Thomas. Now, he realized there was a new level of deception.

"Was this all there was?" Treehorn eyed the personal belongings spread out. "I was told this woman was relocating."

"I would say she was running."

Treehorn pulled on a pair of latex gloves and searched the suitcases. Clothing and normal toiletries. Nothing out of the ordinary for a weekend visit, but definitely not a cross-country move.

Sergeant Peralta emptied the contents of the second evidence box onto the table. It contained financial printouts and a woman's purse.

Numbers covered every line and every space of the papers. Nothing appeared to give the details as to what they represented or their code or cypher.

The detective handed the agent the police file and its photos. "The coroner ruled it an accidental car crash."

"What happened to the Jeep?"

"We still have it in our long-term storage, because I refused to release it."

"You suspected foul play?"

The deputy nodded and handed Treehorn images from the crash.

"I came upon the scene within a few minutes. The Jeep was found facing front into a ditch with its two doors opened. The girl, passenger side, unconscious. I called EMS and put a neck brace on her."

"Is this how you found the car?" Treehorn pointed to the SUV.

"Yes. Its front doors were wide open. The driver, a woman, was deceased."

Treehorn flipped to the next image. A photo showed a woman slumped over the steering wheel.

"Neither airbag had been deployed."

Treehorn looked closer at the colored photographs. No sign of blood, anywhere.

"Here's images from the rear inside of the vehicle. Does that look like a normal crash scene?"

Treehorn looked closely at them. Usually, accidents caused personal belongings to be spread throughout the interior. The suitcases were opened on the rear seat. The clothes appeared pilfered. "Someone searched for something."

"That's my guess. Here's the coroner's report."

Treehorn read the summary. "He ruled Tina died from blunt force trauma?"

"If she did then how did she open her driver's door? I argued for her. Doctor said someone else came upon the scene and checked the victims before I arrived. I say someone reached in and broke her neck."

Treehorn didn't question the seasoned deputy's theory, "Did you interview the girl?"

"Yes, she said she couldn't remember."

"Nothing?" The agent re-examined Cate's image. Her right temple showed a small bruise, but he wondered if it was enough to render her unconscious.

"I asked if they were driven off the road. She didn't know. I asked who opened the doors. She couldn't answer. The ER doctor thought seeing her mother's death may have caused the girl to blackout."

"Plausible."

"I searched her purse and couldn't find anything missing."

Treehorn emptied the contents onto the table. Every item from it was neatly itemized in evidence bags. License, credit cards, and cash all accounted for. No sign of a robbery.

"Did you examine the car once it was impounded?"

"Bumper to bumper but I didn't find anything."

Treehorn examined one last item from the serialized numbered box. An employee laminated identification photo for Tina Dixon from Rathburn Monetary Management. The agent's fingers clenched it as his face flushed in anger. The Fed knew the FBI Director had an agenda when he sent him on this investigation. The question he asked himself, which murder did the director truly want solved?

"Do you know Rathburn?" Deputy Peralta asked upon seeing the agent's response.

"I met him at a few social gatherings. I would like to secure everything here for my investigation, including the printouts."

"My staff can box it all up for you while we examine the vehicle."

Treehorn handed the sheriff's deputy his card. "I agree with you. I think she was running and I think I know from whom."

Deputy Peralta drove the agent to the dark blue Jeep. The SUV appeared intact other than some dirt and grass embedded in the front grill and beneath the bumper.

Treehorn spotted the Rathburn Monetary Management parking lot sticker adhered to the rear side window. No other external damage could be seen.

The deputy unlocked the doors.

Treehorn searched the rear, under the tire storage compartment, and beneath the vehicle. He moved to the rear section and nothing out of the ordinary was found in the door pockets or on the floor. The agent searched the glove compartment between the seats and in the dash. Nothing was amiss.

"I didn't find anything out of the ordinary." Deputy Peralta sounded apologetic.

Treehorn glanced down at the USB media connection. The vehicle had no ashtray so why did the driver have a cigarette lighter? The agent removed it and inside was a hidden USB storage device. He lifted it and showed the deputy.

"I didn't even think of that as a hiding spot."

"Jeep stopped installing cigarette lighters a few years ago."

Deputy Peralta handed the Fed his own business card, "I would appreciate it if you let me know what happens."

"I will." Treehorn placed it into an evidence bag and took an image of it with his camera.

"I'm sorry for failing her. Our agency is swamped here with smuggling up and down the interstate. You can't overrule a coroner."

The deputy transported Treehorn back to his vehicle and assisted him with loading the evidence boxes into his SUV.

When the men completed their document transfer, Deputy Peralta handed Treehorn a sealed manilla envelope with an attached address. "I located Tina's sister's contact information after Cate's death. I'm sorry I couldn't have helped her sooner."

Treehorn didn't question that disclosure. "What's inside?" The agent eyed the sealed document.

"While I waited for the coroner and EMS to arrive at the Dixon's car accident, I quickly fingerprinted the four door handles and a couple of handprints from the rear panels."

Treehorn tilted his head in a silent question.

"I knew one day someone would come and want to solve this case. I never entered them into the system when the coroner ruled the woman's death an accident. Make no mistake, Agent Treehorn, Tina Dixon was murdered."

The Fed needed to see the coroner's report and obtain a second opinion before he would concur. He drove to his hotel so he could examine the USB drive and see what information it contained.

Father Wilkens waved goodbye to a woman from the steps of his church. He observed Thomas in the cemetery standing in front of a gravestone holding a bouquet of flowers.

The priest approached the captain as he placed the flowers gently on his daughter's headstone.

Father Wilkens approached, dressed in his black robe with its white collar, while Thomas stood dressed in black with a white turtleneck.

"Good afternoon, Thomas."

"Father."

They stared solemnly at the engraved granite. 'CATE DIXON. *Beloved daughter of Thomas Brooks, Father and Tina Dixon, Mother. Rest now child, for there are no mysteries, just revelations.*'

Thomas rubbed his daughter's cross. "Cate was buried here before her death was ruled a suicide. Father Bowden came to me. I thought he was offering support." Thomas looked at a nearby tombstone that depicted God with his arms open wide. "He told me that I had to pay for her absolution or remove her body from this sacred place."

"I'm truly sorry." Father Wilkens lowered his head at the incident.

"I went to the rectory to deliver the money. Betty Luzer was ashamed of the church for its greed."

Father Wilkens kept his head lowered as he pictured the events.

"That's when she told me about Father Bowden's diary. I read it cover to cover that day but didn't remove it."

"Did it give you answers you sought?"

"No, but it proved that Father Bowden had personal secrets."

"Did you confront him?" The priest wondered.

"I asked him several times over the course of a year but he always hid behind Canon Law."

"Why did you murder him?"

"I didn't kill him because of the secrets."

"Then why?" Father Wilkens sought the truth.

"I killed him because he threatened my job."

The priest's eyes widened. "What?"

"I grabbed him one day and demanded to know who he protected for the Church."

"He refused to tell." Father Wilkens guessed correctly.

"He told me that he would report my behavior to the Governor's office and that I would lose my job."

"Did he report it?"

Thomas smirked, "I apologized before he made the call. You know the rest."

"Will it make your burden easier to carry?"

Thomas calmly replied, "Yes, and do you know why? This town's residents are going to need your help."

"How would you know that?" The priest asked as a frown marked his brow.

Thomas removed a leather book labeled, *DIARY* from his jacket pocket and handed it to Father Wilkens. "I made a copy and I've removed a few pages to protect the guilty."

The two-hatted priest and lawyer showed no surprise.

Thomas continued with the obvious, "Criminals will commit crimes and sinners will sin. They'll keep us both in business."

Father Wilkens bowed his head in prayer. "I'm cut from two cloths. One of the Church and one of the State."

Thomas looked at the cemetery and then to the town's square, "What do you see when you look at other flocks with envy?"

"That hell has come to this town." Father Wilkens stated with conviction.

"It's always been here." Thomas walked away.

Chapter Fourteen

Do Me A Favor

The special agent stood next to his vehicle checking his emails and messages as Thomas arrived. Treehorn wondered how many skeletons rattled in the captain's closet.

Thomas parked beside him and stepped out of his car. "To what do I owe the pleasure, Agent Treehorn? I thought you and your tail would have scurried back to DC by now."

Treehorn threw his suit jacket onto his front seat and tossed his phone on top of it without commenting.

Thomas raised his eyebrow, smirked, placed his device inside his own vehicle, and shut the door. "Give it your best shot, half-breed."

"After tonight, you're not going to see her again."

"And if I do?"

"I'll return and put a bullet in your head just like you did to Father Bowden and Loveta Chilton."

"Is that a fact?"

Treehorn's lip curled, "You had two problems from the beginning. Do you want to know what they were?"

"Sure." His caustic response grated on Treehorn.

"First, you made a mistake when you killed someone on federal property. Second, FBI Director Andrew Mason assigned the case to me."

Neither man added to the conversation as Melanie arrived and parked next to their vehicles. She climbed out of her car and stared at the two men who were facing off.

Thomas grabbed and kissed her in front of Treehorn, whose face showed slight disapproval. "I have drinks and dinner on the rear seat. Can you put them away, please?"

"Sure." Melanie sat her purse on the hood and reached for the two large bags.

"Agent Hopper, give us a few minutes." Treehorn politely requested.

Melanie raised her eyebrow, "Everything okay?"

"Yes." This time it sounded authoritative.

Thomas added, "Just finalizing the investigations."

Both men waited until she entered the house before speaking again.

Treehorn tapped his gun and then his gold badge with his index finger, *"Thomas Brooks, you have the right to remain silent. Anything you say can and will be used against you in a court of law. You have the right to an attorney. If you cannot afford an attorney, one will be*

266

provided for you. Do you understand the rights I have just read to you?"

"Yes." Thomas chuckled.

"With these rights in mind, do you wish to speak to me?"

Thomas examined Treehorn's flat shirt pockets. "Yes. I'm more than happy to answer any of your questions, but I have one for you first. Do you have a recording device on you?"

"No." Treehorn pulled out his pants pockets to show that they were empty. The only thing in his hand was a Chevy Tahoe key fob.

"You owe me a question and I wish to collect."

"Go ahead."

"Why did Tina Dixon run from you when she was pregnant?"

"She scurried away when she realized I wasn't father material. She's lucky she's dead, because I would have found her and killed her for leaving me when she carried my kid in her belly."

"She saw your other side one day and she knew she had to escape."

"You'll never know, will you? Unless she left a diary of my secrets."

"Why did you shoot Father Bowden and Loveta Chilton?"

Thomas looked to his house to make sure Melanie wasn't listening.

Treehorn stood stoic as he met the face of a cold hard killer.

"When did you suspect me?" Thomas curiosity asked.

"Or, when did I know?" Treehorn parried. "I suspected when my supervisor informed me that you were friends with the Director. I knew when I interviewed Winter LaGrange and realized you had picked up her phone instead of her mothers. You were in the rectory when Winter arrived with the groceries and while she went to the bathroom."

"I made a mistake."

"Why did you mail me the phone?"

"You can't convict a man if he doesn't have the evidence."

"Why kill Loveta?"

"I didn't know what the priest had told her about me. A victim of circumstance."

Treehorn returned to the primary question in his case, "Why did you kill Father Bowden?"

Thomas smiled. The emotion didn't reach his eyes. "That dirty priest threatened my job after a confrontation. The same way your director's going to threaten yours when you return to DC."

Treehorn's upper lip curled in disgust.

"It's your word against mine." Thomas knew the reality of their conversation.

"Did Major Morgan know of your dirty deeds?"

Thomas shook his head, "No. He's a good man. We rose the ranks together but he's completely in the dark."

"Tell me about your relationship with FBI Director Andrew Mason."

"We're friends from the Academy. We talk weekly and I'm the godfather to his oldest son."

"What part of the puzzle am I missing?" Treehorn grilled.

"He assigned you here on purpose. You weren't getting a conviction for murder and it would be a stain on your record."

"You didn't know that the church was on federal property? A little unknown fact."

"No, that was definitely an error on my part. I telephoned Andrew when I got home. He said he'd fix everything by assigning you to the case. We laughed about how you conducted your investigation: your little bulletin boards and everything in plain sight. We spoke about you and your little protegee, just two half-breeds that didn't have a clue."

The two men heard the front door slam.

Thomas observed Treehorn's lack of action, "So, why are you not pulling out your handcuffs, Mr. Treehorn?"

"I'm not taking you in and it's Special Agent John Treehorn." He spat.

Melanie shook her head at the two men as she searched her purse on the hood. "Treehorn, have you seen my phone?"

"It's in my vehicle where you dropped it."

"Why didn't you tell me?"

"Doing your job means keeping track of your FBI equipment."

Melanie walked away in a huff.

Thomas watched her rear as she went to the passenger side of Treehorn's vehicle to retrieve her device.

Treehorn eyed Thomas in further disgust.

Thomas whispered to Treehorn. "You never wanted that?"

A flash of anger crossed Treehorn's face on how he treated Melanie. The agent tapped his pistol. "Say goodbye to her." He turned and walked to his vehicle as his silver FBI issued handcuffs caught Thomas's eye, shining on the man's belt.

"Did you forget something, *Agent* Treehorn? My arrest?"

Treehorn looked back. "I didn't forget a thing."

Melanie waved her phone and walked over and dropped it in her purse. "Let me say good-bye to him."

Thomas nodded and watched the pair.

Treehorn yanked open his driver's door as Melanie caught up to him.

Nikki Costa's song played through her earbuds wrapped around her neck, but loud enough that Treehorn heard the title, *'Everybody Got Their Something.'*

Treehorn climbed into his vehicle.

Melanie glanced at Thomas. "Thanks for looking the other way."

"Did I?" Treehorn whispered it so softly the hairs stood to attention on Melanie's neck.

"I'll see you later."

"Don't miss your flight." Treehorn reminded her.

Melanie smirked, "I did my job. We got a sexual predator from Altona off the street."

"No, our job was to catch Father Bowden's killer." He then slammed his SUV door a little harder than usual.

Thomas and Melanie watched as Treehorn peeled out of the driveway.

"Is that man ever happy?"

"No." Melanie chuckled and then took a long hard look at Thomas. "We're not seeing each other again, are we?"

"No. Your partner left detailed instructions."

Melanie snorted.

"He made a slight threat."

Melanie burst out in laughter.

"What's so funny?"

"Treehorn doesn't make threats. He keeps promises."

Thomas glanced at the Tahoe in the distance and then at Melanie.

"I brought us food and drinks, too."

Thomas lost his smile as Melanie turned towards the bungalow wearing her gun and badge as she carried two small bags from her SUV.

"Can you grab my bag, please?"

Thomas glanced inside the agent's open purse on his car hood. Her powered down phone, two bullet magazines, tissue, and her keys lay visible. Nothing else. He grabbed her bag and grinned.

"I'm grateful my daughter's rapist was apprehended and your partner's concluded his investigation."

Melanie smiled as he spoke.

"You can't win them all." Thomas jested.

Melanie stopped and faced the man. "There's something you don't know about that very *Special Agent*."

"What's that?"

"Treehorn doesn't stop. If someone makes a single mistake, he won't let you forget it. Trust me, I know."

Thomas raised an eyebrow.

"He's never closed a case until he's believed that it's been solved. The killer will need to look over his shoulder for the rest of his life because my partner won't stop."

"Is that right?"

Melanie turned serious, "I'm sorry Treehorn couldn't solve Father Bowden's and Loveta Chilton's deaths, today."

"There's no statute of limitations on murder."

"Treehorn knows that. When you turn away from him, you'll see his shadow that's covered you. When you think he's gone, he'll return and strike."

Thomas leaned down and kissed Melanie. "I'll remember that." Words of wisdom one atoned for as he carried her purse inside.

The miles sped by for FBI Special Agent John Treehorn. On his passenger seat sat his phone on his jacket while Agent Hopper's digital voice recorder peeked out from beneath.

Hours later as Thomas washed his hands in the bathroom, he heard Melanie's SUV drive away. She left a single word note on the kitchen table for him, *"Goodbye."* He walked to his front door and watched as her red tail lights disappeared into the night.

He petted the little rust colored tabby cat that slept curled in his chair. The log crackled in the fireplace as he walked to its above mantel and looked at the photographs of his daughter that lined it. He took his time as he examined each of them and he felt nothing for the stranger in the pictures.

Thomas pressed a camouflaged button. A hidden door opened and allowed him access to a secret room. Inside, a wall full of documents lined the wall. It was similar to Treehorn's investigative bulletin board, but this was not a murder board. Instead, it displayed a listing of current events. Joseph Granger's headline took center stage: *Accused Rapist Denied Bail* followed by *Same Gun Builds and Destroys Church*. An image of St. Philomena's Church and a superimposed image of Gardenia Myers. *Town Historian Exposed as Voyeur and Blackmailer*. The last one was for Dooley Stiles, *Judge Stiles Investigated For Blackmail*. The last clipping had Thomas raising his whiskey glass, *No Arrests for Double Murders*. He knew evil begets evil.

Meanwhile, Joseph Granger lay huddled on his cot as the sounds of prison activity echoed within its unit. The lamps dimmed three times that signified nightly lights out for bedtime. A prison guard jingled his keys as he walked past Granger's cell. Darkness shuttered the building and then night safety lanterns turned on. A sound of a key being inserted into Joseph's cell door caused the prisoner to break out in a sweat. The bars opened and closed. Someone had entered, "Nice."

The sound of Joseph's cries filled the room.

The deputy whispered, "My name is Mark Porter and I'm here to take care of you." The guard rattled his keys near the man's ears. "My desk is right outside. Your door will remain unlocked at night, just like you forced Cate Dixon to leave her window unlocked. You'll feel right at home."

Lightning illuminated the tiny prison window as the guard slipped away, rattling his keys, and whistling a catchy tune.

Thomas now examined the second wall in his secret den. A short, brief note sent to him from Betty Luzer, Father Bowden's retired housekeeper, now deceased. *"I've asked my lawyer to send you this package upon my death. Father Bowden knows who raped Cate Dixon. There's a diary of confessions in his night stand. It may help you to find justice for her. I've sent you the gun the girl used to commit suicide and a knife which he kept in his safe. May God forgive me."*

Thomas examined another pinned document on his board. It's the top half of a torn diary page that was stabbed to Father Bowden's body. It stated, *"I have committed a crime. A crime against my God, my church, and my community. Please forgive me."* The bottom half of a page is now taped to it. The torn edges lined up. The priest's words written so long ago read, *"Thomas made this statement to me today. He told me that I would understand tomorrow night after he sins. No one can premeditate their confessions."*

Thomas looked at his watch. It was almost 8 pm as he turned off the lights and closed his secret room. He placed another log on the fire and settled into his comfortable chair to absorb its warmth. The man who would never forget how a community treated him opened a book labeled, *DIARY*. Cate's cross and gold chain provided the bookmark for its last written entry.

A sound activated reel-to-reel recorder turned on. The church music gently played in the background, '*Onward Christian Soldier'*.

Thomas stared at the blank page and waited.

The distant sound of a door squeaking on much needed to be oiled hinges could be heard.

Then, someone's footsteps neared.

The *'devil's doorbell'* rang on the confessional booth and then the unique sound of its entrance squeaking as it opened and closed.

Father Wilken's voice is heard, "May the Lord be in our heart to help you make a good confession."

A stranger's voice replied, "Bless me, Father, for I have sinned. It has been seven days since my last confession. These are my sins."

Thomas's pencil scratched the paper's surface as the living room clock cuckooed.

Treehorn sat alone in a departure area of the Plattsburgh International Airport.

Melanie plopped down next to him, "Why do you choose to fly at night?"

Treehorn sighed. "I can either stay awake at the hotel or on an airplane. Since you hate to fly, you can catch some sleep during the flight."

"I could have flown to Detroit tomorrow."

The loudspeaker announced Treehorn's flight to Washington. He stood and removed a warrant from his breast pocket and handed it to his partner.

Melanie readily accepted it.

"It's best for you to be away from him."

"Says the lonely man."

Treehorn's concern vanished, "Do your job." As he strode away, he missed Melanie's mocking salute to his back.

Chapter Fifteen

Do Your Job

Sunday morning found Treehorn knocking on the door of a historic row house in Arlington, Virginia. The names Pauline Peterson and Rene Gagnon were clearly printed on the black antique mailbox.

A woman in her early forties answered the man when he rang her doorbell. "Agent Treehorn?"

"Yes." He nodded and presented his identification for her inspection.

"Come in." She opened her front door which allowed him to enter. "How do you take your coffee?"

"Black." The agent wasn't given an option.

"Have a seat."

As the woman poured their drinks, Treehorn noticed the twin Georgetown University Law Degree diplomas hung on the wall, one for her and the other for her husband.

"I'm not sure I understand why you are here, Agent Treehorn."

The man searched the woman's eyes, lawyer to lawyer, looking for a resemblance to her sister. Before he could answer, she continued.

"You're not the first FBI agent to cross that threshold asking about Tina. Why should I answer any of your questions?"

"Your sister's case was listed as a car accident. But, was it? Your tone implies you have information."

Score one for the FBI.

Pauline tilted her head. "Why don't you give me your opinion first—from what you've learned in the short time you've investigated my sister."

Treehorn took a sip of the coffee. His eye contact didn't waver and neither did hers.

"Thomas Brooks is evil. Your sister ran from him after she became pregnant, because she understood he wasn't father material."

"Correct."

"Your sister worked for Rathburn Monetary Management as an accountant."

"Correct, again."

"Jules Rathburn set her up with a fake identity and security in Albuquerque to keep her and her daughter safe."

"Your FBI agents knew that, too."

"She was a valued employee—until she uncovered something." Treehorn made a supposition.

Pauline neither confirmed nor denied it.

"That put her in jeopardy, again. She ran, taking the proof with her." Treehorn theorized after seeing the documents and USB drive in his possession.

The woman's face showed no emotion.

"I would guess someone from Rathburn showed up immediately after her disappearance, questioning you about her whereabouts."

Again, silence from the lawyer.

"As you know, I met with Essex County Deputy Peralta."

She waited for the agent to hit paydirt.

"I don't believe your sister was heading to see Thomas nor to Rathburn's New York office. I think she was heading to you and your husband's second home in Montreal."

"Very good, Agent Treehorn. She needed a safe place to hide. The only problem with that plan was we agreed on *no communication.*"

"You didn't know about the car accident?"

"No. They contacted the next of kin, being her fake husband, Kyle Dixon. Deputy Peralta dug deeper and found me. By that time, Tina was dead."

Sadness clouded the woman's eyes.

"Did Deputy Peralta tell you he suspected foul play?"

"Yes, but neither of your agents cared about my sister. The older one arrived asking specific questions about Jules Rathburn's activities in DC, while the younger one showed up a few days later questioning the man's financial activities."

"What were their names?"

"FBI Assistant Director Leo Mancuso and Agent Benjamin Latimer."

The only outward sign Treehorn exhibited was the whitening of his knuckles as he clenched his coffee cup. "I read Tina's autopsy report last night and I agree with the sheriff's deputy. I also believe your sister's manner of death was suspicious, due to the mitigating circumstances. Would you allow me to exhume her body and have her re-examined by my staff? You have my promise that I will not stop searching until I find the answers."

Ms. Peterson stood up from her table. Treehorn did, too.

The woman took a long look at the special agent. "Yes, I'll give you permission." She then opened her purse, removed something and rubbed it between her fingers while lost in a memory. Finally, she handed Treehorn a brass item.

He examined the postal key with a number engraved on it.

"Tina asked me to set her up a box several years ago, when she first started to have suspicions that something wasn't right at work. I don't know what's in it, but I'm hoping that it will help you find answers. It's at Dunn Loring."

Treehorn gave a slight nod.

"And, as a lawyer, I would recommend that you don't tell anyone. It's obvious that your fellow agents have their own agendas that don't seem to include my sister."

Pauline accompanied Treehorn to her front door. "Here's my business card. I'll wait for the cemetery paperwork from you. I would like updates when they become available."

Treehorn handed her his information, "Count on it."

The agent walked to his vehicle and searched his telephone contacts.

Later, Everett Abbott from the United States Postal Inspection Service met Treehorn at the Dunn Loring postal branch in Virginia. A burly bushy eyebrowed man waited.

"You couldn't wait until tomorrow to pick up your mail?" He joked.

"Murder investigation."

"You've got a warrant?"

"I have a key."

"That's even better."

The inspector unlocked the door and relocked it after they entered.

"Sorry, I missed our last couple of poker nights."

"Duty calls. Everett eyed Treehorn's fading black and blue marks. "Heard through the grapevine you left some bruises on Shady Lynch."

"I'll take the fifth on that."

"The LEOs decided to donate all of their next winnings to your charity of choice in Shady's name." The postal inspector chuckled as he tried to extract a response from the Navajo agent, but all he received was the slight lift of the man's lip. He considered that a win.

Treehorn reached the designated extra-large box and inserted its key. He opened it wearing latex gloves and had evidence bags ready. Manila envelopes filled the interior space to capacity. Treehorn removed each one glancing at their postage date and the return sender's name, before placing it in its own bag and labeling it. Not a single envelope had Tina Dixon's name on it. At the very bottom of the stack lay a large, thick, white envelope that had

Thomas Brooks name in the return address section, but was written by a feminine cursive hand. Its postal stamp showed that it was sent from New Mexico five years ago.

"Looks like these will keep you busy for quite some time."

"I'm in luck. There's no statute of limitations on murder."

"This is true."

The two men left the building.

"Will we see you Wednesday?" Everett asked.

"If I'm in town, I'll be there with my donation."

Treehorn went into his office on Sunday afternoon and dropped off his case notes and closure document. That evening, the agent stood in his den and examined the documents spread out in evidence bags. Each one meticulously documented, detailed, and categorized. The agent now realized the scope of both Mancuso and Agent Benjamin Latimer's investigations. Tina Dixon's ex-boss Jules Rathburn held one key. FBI Director Andrew Mason held another. FBI Special Agent John Treehorn held a third, derived from Tina Dixon's USB storage device.

Treehorn arrived early in Washington from his Georgetown home so he could stop at his favorite coffee cart and grab two coffees from the mobile barista. His long legs carried him into his FBI office at the J. Edgar Hoover building. Agents, staff, and strangers alike parted for him as he strode to the elevator. No one slowed his progress this morning.

Lucky for him, an agent was exiting the door as he entered so he could sneak up on the office administrator.

"Hello Abby." He sat the two coffees on the counter.

She turned and the smile on her face brightened his day. For once, she forgot professional etiquette and gave him a hug which he gladly returned.

"Welcome back. We missed you at your party, you know the one you avoided."

"I'm sorry, a murderer awaited."

"Justice?"

"One day."

She rubbed his eyebrow where the catgut stitch had been.

"How's it look?"

"Like the warrior's returned." Abby said, in all seriousness.

The agent winked.

"Your dessert's in the freezer." She leaned into his space, "You *can* have your cake and eat it, too."

Treehorn smiled.

"Thanks for the coffee and the big guy wants to see you."

The agent picked up his drink and accepted the messages Abby handed to him. "Thanks for being my partner while I was away."

"Hilda contacted you from Communications. Her message is on top. I'll give you a heads up. *She's not happy.*"

"I'll call her after the meeting. Thanks, Abby."

The administrator took the time to watch her favorite agent walk down the hallway as the staff stepped aside for him. They knew who the boss was.

Treehorn sat his coffee and messages on his desk, then hurried to the FBI director's plush office, up on the 11th floor.

Lydia, the director's administrator, sat in front of her computer.

"Good morning."

"And good morning to you, John. You can go right in. They're waiting for you."

Treehorn nodded and then crossed the threshold into FBI Director Andrew Mason's office. In front of the wooden desk where J. Edgar Hoover used to conduct business sat his supervisor: Leo Mancuso.

"Close the door." The agent complied and took an empty seat.

No litter cluttered the desk. A telephone sat on the left, a *Rules & Regulations* book on the right and a single, open folder beneath the directors hands.

Mancuso took one look at Treehorn's near faded bruises, "Welcome back."

The agent nodded, then observed his boss tapping his middle finger on his pant leg. The universal sign for, *"You're so screwed."*

Director Mason started, "I see you telephoned Rathburn Monetary Management regarding Tina Dixon."

"Background employment history. As I noted, their Human Resources Department stated she resigned from her job. They added that she was a valued employee in their accounting division and had offered her employment in their New York branch but she had declined. Was there something I needed to recheck?"

"No, that section appears satisfactory. Let's focus on your job. There were some errors on your closure report."

"Sir?"

The director held up a document.

"Your friend, Captain Thomas Brooks, committed two murders."

"I corrected your statement."

"It's totally accurate."

"I disagree."

Treehorn squinted. "I have the telephone that your friend, Captain Brooks, removed from a murder scene. Second, there's Agent Hopper's voice recorder where, once again, your friend accepted being Mirandized and confessed to the killings."

"So, why didn't you arrest him?"

"I listened to the device, verified his statement, and documented the evidence for the referral to the federal DA's office. Those two things will indict him."

"Do you know what's missing from this report?"

"Nothing's missing."

"Yes, your signature."

"Sir?"

"Here's the statement you'll sign." The director handed Treehorn a paper and shredded the original.

The agent examined it. "You're ordering me to sign a falsified statement." Treehorn read the legal document and his brow creased more with each passage. "There's no mention of the telephone or Brook's confession. We have the evidence." Treehorn's voice rose in anger.

The director stood, opened his desk drawer like a magician, reached into its depth, and lifted two items in serialized evidence bags. Winter LaGrange's telephone and Agent Hopper's digital recorder. The head of the FBI, once again, reached for something in the bowels of his drawer. He grabbed a hammer and brought it down on the two devices that lay on the thick book. He continued to smash them until they broke into several pieces.

Treehorn stood with fists, clenched.

The director calmly tossed the hammer back into its drawer and slammed it closed. He tossed the two bags to Mancuso who, wisely in the circumstances, kept his mouth shut.

"Director Mason, you just destroyed evidence in a murder investigation." Treehorn angrily pointed at him.

The director didn't comment on the man's outburst, but instead looked at the Special Agent and calmly stated, "Sign the closure document so we can move on."

Treehorn's gaze traveled from the head of his agency to his supervisor, the Assistant Director.

Mancuso looked down to avoid his agent's eye, "Sign the document John, so we can put this incident behind us."

"You're asking me to sign a statement that Director Mason falsified. You're asking me to cover up a double-murder confession."

"Yes." Mancuso stated matter-of-factly.

The director snapped, "You should have taken better care of evidence in your possession, Agent Treehorn. Now, sign the document."

Treehorn looked at the FBI pen that Mancuso handed him. The words engraved on its side, *Fidelity, Bravery, and Integrity*. He had two options: He could comply with the illegal action or be fired. A piece of Treehorn broke at that moment. The agent hesitated, then with an unsteady hand, he scrawled his signature on the paper. He callously tossed the pen on the desk and turned towards the door to make his escape.

"Sit down!" The director yelled. "We're not finished." The man then casually picked up the paper, examined it, placed it in the folder, and handed it all to Mancuso. "I'll see you later, Leo, at our budget meeting." Mason pointed him to the exit.

Leo stood, walked out, and softly closed the door.

The two men stared at each other across the antique desk.

Treehorn's face flushed in anger.

"I didn't think you could turn that red, being a half-breed. Your face looks like a full-blooded Native." Mason chuckled and then watched his agent's demeanor change.

Treehorn assessed his options and stayed silent.

"Do you know what your problem is, Agent Treehorn? You think like an agent and not as a criminal. Everything for you is justice." The director watched the cold and calculating agent he had known for years reappear before his eyes.

Treehorn's clenched jaw kept him from speaking.

"I'm going to let this little incident slide. You see, Thomas Brooks is my friend. Has been since the academy. He called me after he murdered the priest and housekeeper. He didn't know that little piece of land was federal property but the coroner, who happened to be a history buff, did. By morning I had the facts and assigned you the case."

Treehorn waited for an end to the man's diatribe.

"Consider the case cold and closed. Just like your persona."

Treehorn needed to learn this man's endgame, "You sent me there to solve the murder, so you could bury it."

Mason slammed his hand down on the desk, "See, that's justice. You're neither slow nor stupid, Agent Treehorn."

"And, to find the details on Rathburn's connection."

All humor disappeared from the director's face.

"I didn't give a rat's ass about those two murders. The priest deserved it for hiding his rapist son. The housekeeper was in the wrong place at the wrong time. She's nobody."

"You needed to know what I would uncover on Jules Rathburn."

"Exactly. You know what else? I killed two birds with one stone. Thomas is free from a future murder charge. Rathburn has no connection to his ex-employee, and now, I'm ordering you never to go anywhere near him. Consider that a direct and permanent order. That's an itch you will never scratch as long as I'm sitting in this chair."

"His justice will come with the truth."

"Maybe, but not today. We have the law and you will follow it. I've yet to figure out what Mancuso sees in you but you know what? I don't care. Now, get the hell out of my office."

The agent took one long look at the director and walked out, leaving his door hanging wide open.

Treehorn walked directly to the Assistant Director's office.

Patricia, Mancuso's administrator greeted the agent. "Good morning. You and the A.D. should coordinate your activities."

"Good morning, and why's that?"

"Because, he's waiting for you in your office."

"Thanks, Patricia."

The administrator watched the agent's long stride disappear from sight. She sighed, and resumed her typing.

Leo Mancuso examined Treehorn's University of Arizona Law Degree framed on his wall. He remembered it because he was there for him and one other.

The agent closed his door. "That was a good day." As he too looked at his diploma.

"Yes, it was. Drink your coffee before it gets too cold."

"You can't be an FBI agent if you don't like it at room temperature."

"This is true."

Treehorn opened his safe while Leo settled into the chair.

Assistant Director Mancuso glanced at the neatly organized desk with its two pictures in the corner. One of his parents as he was sworn in as an FBI agent and the other his deceased wife.

The agent removed the box from his safe and his lip lifted. Abby had wrapped it like a gift.

Mancuso voiced his sentiment, "Fidelity, bravery, and integrity. Do you think we value one over the others? You were brave to sign that document while the director lost his integrity. Asking an agent to break the law?" He sighed. "So, I would say fidelity is our backbone."

Treehorn glanced at the photograph of his parents. It was the day he'd become an FBI agent. He believed it was one's loyalty to one's self that knew the difference between law and justice.

"Sometimes, it's a high price that we pay." Mancuso tapped the bulging envelope that sat on top of Bowden's case file. He emptied it and two smashed items slid out: a cellphone and Agent Hopper's digital recorder. "Here's your original closure report, unsigned."

Treehorn signed it without examining it. As if it was the plan all along.

Mancuso held out his hand, palm up to Treehorn.

The agent reached into his pants pocket and removed a digital recorder that was labeled, *Andrew Mason*.

Mancuso hit rewind, the clear sound of a hammer smashing could be heard and then Treehorn's voice, *"Director Mason, you just destroyed evidence in a murder investigation."* Assistant Director Mancuso shut off the device and dropped it into the envelope. Then, he removed the falsified report from its folder, the one Treehorn signed on Hoover's desk, and placed that inside. He added the two evidence bags with their smashed pieces. "I would suggest you secure this where no one will find it in the near foreseeable future."

Treehorn accepted the packaged contents and asked, "Why did you speak to Pauline Peterson?"

"I needed to know what the director knew in DC. It appeared to be a dead end."

"Why did Special Agent Benjamin Latimer question her?"

"You're not slow to this song and dance, John."

"Did you know that Shady interviewed Ms. Peterson? He had to use his real identification to enter a lawyer's house."

"He doesn't pull that badge out often."

"More like never." Treehorn reckoned. "Mason ordered me to stay away from Rathburn, but what about Shady's activities?"

Mancuso stood. "When did you know?"

Treehorn met Mancuso's eyes, "Know what? That Shady never resigned from the FBI? That he's been an undercover CIA agent? Using his father's name given to him, Benito Del Toro in Mexico and Shady Lynch here in the States?"

"I don't believe Shady would have disclosed that."

Treehorn didn't give his supervisor an answer. "Shady didn't leave the FBI quietly, did he? I would say he's been working on one goal all of these years."

Mancuso said nothing.

"When Shady returned on that Monday, following our graduation from the academy, he informed me that he had resigned from the FBI after meeting with you." Treehorn eyed his boss. "He offered no explanation."

"He didn't owe you one." Mancuso replied.

"True, but you just confirmed what I've suspected from that day."

Mancuso stayed silent.

"You see, Shady didn't agree with your deal, even if you believed that. He whispered two words to me as he walked away. A clue to his agenda which I've never forgotten. Do you want to take a guess at whose name he gave?"

Mancuso's eyes showed secrets he wouldn't share.

"Did you think it was his step-father, Jules Rathburn?"

The Assistant Director refused to guess.

Treehorn's lip curled. "You would be wrong." He continued, "So, you see, I don't need to be on Rathburn's case, when we both know that's Shady's endgame."

Mancuso offered a suggestion. "Shady needs to identify the one person who's pulling the strings. Rathburn, or the Director, because from my observation, someone has a skeleton in their closet that's trying to escape."

Treehorn understood his supervisor's implication.

Mancuso handed his agent the Bowden case file.

"I read over the file and found something missing."

"What?" asked Treehorn.

"You didn't mention Agent Hopper's trip to Detroit."

"I didn't want the evidence she gathered to be destroyed."

"Which is?"

"I sent her to OnStar headquarters to pull the original data from Thomas Brooks' vehicle the night of the murders and his subsequent criminal activities."

"Was she successful?"

"Yes. Nailed his coffin."

"Add it to the file and then close this investigation. That's an order."

"I also found Tina Dixon's death suspicious. I didn't mention that in the file."

"Open a separate investigation but do it, *quietly*. By the way, how's Agent Shelly?"

"He was fine when we spoke during the week."

"Well, tell Raven to stop hacking my server or get better at it. This time, I let him see what I wanted him to see."

The agent didn't refute it. "And Thomas Brooks?"

Mancuso opened the door, "Do me a favor, Agent Treehorn."

"What's that?"

"Do your job..." Mancuso examined his FBI watch, the one engraved with fidelity, bravery, and integrity, "...and have a safe flight to New York."

The agent nodded as the assistant director walked away.

Treehorn packaged Mancuso's bulging envelope into a shipping box. He would mail it to his mother on the Navajo Indian Reservation for safe keeping.

He telephoned Hilda in his communications department while he opened Abby's gift-wrapped package.

"Tech Garland."

"Agent Treehorn."

"Can you tell me why you sent me a dud telephone and then Director Mason removed it?" Hilda demanded.

Treehorn told her the truth, "I needed to know if our Director was dirty."

"I'll assume you got your answer. So, what happened to the telephone I traced?"

Treehorn opened Abby's *gift*. Inside sat Winter LaGrange's cellphone that Captain Thomas Brooks had so arrogantly mailed to him. "I have it secured. Enjoy your retirement, Hilda."

The agent then stood up and removed Agent Hopper's digital recorder device from his pocket, a twin to the one Director Mason had smashed. Treehorn thought back to Saturday when Agent Hopper went to his vehicle to retrieve her telephone, as planned. She had left hidden beneath his suit jacket on its front seat, not one device, but two, after she had recorded Thomas Brooks confessing to his crimes.

Treehorn telephoned Sally Vance, the Federal District Attorney in New York, and scheduled a meeting for the next day. Abby arranged his flight.

He poured himself a fresh coffee and ate his cake.

A week later, the investigation hit the news, *Today, a grand jury out of the Federal District Court of Southern New York indicted New York State Police Captain Thomas Brooks on two counts of murder for the deaths of Father Howard Bowden and Loveta Chilton of Altona, NY. The Governor's office released a statement after the indictment, "No New York State Police officer is above the law. Mr. Brook's employment has been terminated. We thank FBI Director Andrew Mason who couldn't be here today." Special Agent John Treehorn was credited as lead investigator. —Jori Lansing reporting for the Indian Times.*

Later that day, Agent Treehorn received *thank you messages* from Stella Hunter, Father Wilkens, and Eleanor Humphrey. In addition, Winter LaGrange called to thank him for returning the data stored on her phone and finding justice for her mother.

Treehorn's device beeped with a text from Melanie, "Are you happy, Buddha?"

He smiled and replied, "Thanks for doing your job, grasshopper."

She typed, "Don't forget it."

Treehorn wouldn't, nor would he be allowed to forget the fact that he had made an enemy of the FBI Director.

THE END

The next John Treehorn Mystery, RAILROAD CROSSING, a #1 best-seller, is available on Amazon.

RAILROAD CROSSING A John Treehorn Mystery (Book 6 Short Read #2) FBI Special Agent John Treehorn investigates a murder of a psychiatrist on the Navajo Indian Reservation who treated military veterans who suffered from post-traumatic stress disorders. Horrific memories emerge for both the agent and killer when the case takes a deadly turn. No amount of justice can stop the pain of their survival. All royalties go to veterans charity.

SHADOW DANCER (Book 1) 'A victim never forgets.' A dead man's clue sends FBI Special Agent John Treehorn, to the Land of his People, the Navajo Indian Reservation, to hunt an elusive murderer named 'Shadow Dancer' the same Indian myth who once brought this decorated law enforcement officer to his knees.

STOLEN SISTERS (Book 2) 'Death wears a red dress.' FBI Special Agent John Treehorn arrives in an isolated oil boomtown after a wolf uncovers a woman's frozen hand grasping an FBI badge and a final request, "Call FBI Agent John Treehorn". He doesn't know the victim or why she summoned him, but he answers her call. As Treehorn hunts for the Navajo engineer's killer, his fellow agent Raven Shelly searches for a missing prostitute in the same crime-afflicted town. When a red dress worn by one woman is found to belong to the other, the two cases merge as one, thus confirming Treehorn's suspicion that there's a serial killer who walks among them and the agent intends to bury him.

BAD PENNY (Book 3, Short Read #1) FBI Special Agent John Treehorn investigates a murder of an Indian

Posse member who was killed by a gun by one of two Indians standing over his body. All royalties go to charity.

INDIAN POSSE (Book 4) 'Justice, she'll never be denied.' FBI Special Agent John Treehorn hunts a killer on the Navajo Indian Reservation who murdered two members of Indian Posse, a ruthless gang who hunts criminals who failed to pay their debts to society.

Made in the USA
Monee, IL
18 May 2020